PAY WHAT IT'S WORTH

PAY WHAT IT'S WORTH

You Don't Need to Set a Price on Value

TARA JOYCE

#PAYWHATITSWORTH

Join the Pay What It's Worth conversation by using the hashtag #PayWhatItsWorth and/or #PWIW on social media.

Check in on my Pay What It's Worth journey by visiting paywhatitsworth.com.

First printing 2020 by Integral Publishers LLC.

ISBN 978-1-77180-604-6 (paperback)
ISBN 978-1-77180-603-9 (epub)

This is an original print edition of *Pay What It's Worth*.

For DEB,
Your love turns me on.

"In Nature, the price is always charged; always collected; always paid. Often it is paid in advance; again, at the time of delivery (C.O.D.); again, after the delivery, sometimes long after; perhaps in future installments. But the price is always paid, in one way or another."[1]

Law of Balance and Compensation, *The Kybalion*

CONTENTS

ACTION

VALUABLE WORDS

Every new approach requires a language and logic that will accurately represent its ideas, define its values and terms, and ensure a common understanding. These words—and the shared meaning we give to them—are key to understanding and practicing Pay What It's Worth.

Abundance: a perspective on life that acknowledges the wealth of resources a human being has access to.

Accountability: to be responsible to the consequences of your choices and actions.

Business: two parties choosing to be in an exchange of value with each other.

Co-create: to access, activate and express our ability to shape our reality and our world, through our energy, thoughts, feelings, words, and actions.

Communication: the interplay of language, logic, feelings, actions, and energy expressed externally.

Connection: to share a sense of value and respect.

Disclosure: the open sharing of relevant facts and information.

Economy: the environment in which you exchange that which you value.

Exchange: the act of giving and receiving, facilitated by a shared connection.

Generosity: the act of opening, releasing, and allowing; a recognition of the equality and interdependence of all.

Norms: clear and well-founded rules and boundaries for behaviour.

Product: what is given and received in an exchange; a creation of your work and business.

Stakeholder: one who has a vested interest in something.

System: a natural way of organizing things that exchange value and share a common connection.

Value: the worth of something; what is exchanged in a business transaction.

Worth: a personal determination of the importance and care you place on something/someone/yourself.

WHY PAY
WHAT IT'S WORTH?

Explore Your Relationships

At its core, this is a business book about marketing your values, and employing pricing as a means to do so. More importantly though, this is a book that explores business as a tool for extending *who you are through what you do.* I call this approach to business "Innerpreneurship"—business ownership as a vehicle for personal fulfillment and satisfaction *through* work.[2] If this sounds like you and/or you can stay open to exploring business and business ownership in this form—as a tool for material, emotional, intellectual, and spiritual growth—you will receive the most value from this book and this exploration of Pay What It's Worth pricing. Because not setting prices is more than a business strategy, it is also a way of consciously exploring your relationship to money, to other people, and to exchanging value. In order to prosper without setting prices, you need to understand *why* you do business—and *how* you're communicating this value to others.

Market Your Value(s)

As I began to practice with and employ my own system of not setting prices, it became clear to me that one of the easiest aspects of the approach was getting my customer to pay. We, as a collective culture, understand there is a price to pay for the things we need. However, what we're less clear about—and connected to—is our needs around fairness and balance in these exchanges. It is (and was) a very real challenge to support my customer in being fair and balanced in their giving, and in turn, to be fair and balanced in mine. Money is perceived as power, and this idea is so ingrained it can be difficult to see the ways in which we unconsciously wield it. As my understanding of human nature matured, I found myself focusing on how I could create exchanges that were consistently and reliably *mutually* beneficial. This was the only way not setting prices could be sustainable and realistic for my business. I saw communications and/or intentions like "pay what you can" and "pay what you want" disempowering, helping to create an inequitable power-relationship between the buyer and the seller. The language and logic communicated is one of scarcity on behalf of the customer or the creator. In neither communication are the buyer and seller equal. "Pay what you can" is a power-over statement, communicating the parameters for the exchange is about the customer and their lack (and the seller's agreement to receive less). Using the words "what you can," communicates subtlety that I perceive you are in lack and I set an expectation that your neediness is the key factor of the exchange. This type of communication works if you are a not-for-profit organization, but if you are seeking to sustainably profit in your business, it's not a strong choice. Conversely, "pay what you want" is a power-under statement, communicating the parameters of the exchange are about the seller and their lack (and the focus of the exchange is on the wants of the customer alone). Using the words "what you want," communicates subtlety that I perceive I am in lack and I set an expectation that your desires are the important factor of the exchange. More importantly, neither of these intentions and/or communications infers the need for a fair and mutually beneficial exchange of value. Neither approach allows buyer AND seller to be empowered to enter the exchange as equals, or to take shared responsibility for the relationship. I realized that for a sustainable exchange to be created, value needed to be mutually given and received. Both participants needed to be responsible to fairly valuing the contributions of the exchange. It is this intention—for mutual fulfillment and responsibility—that moves the strategy of not setting prices beyond a sales tactic and pricing strategy, and towards a viable system for valuing your business, your offerings, your customer, and maybe even the world. When social responsibility is shared, not setting prices is more than a counter-pricing method, it is a cutting-edge, progressive, and sustainable model for doing business.

I've come to call this socially responsible system for not setting prices, "Pay What It's Worth" (I also use the acronym, "PWIW"). I use the specific words "Pay," "It," and "Worth" in my language as I've found it's extremely important to consider and clearly communicate what I am asking my customer to do in our exchange, and to model that behaviour myself. If I want my customer to fairly determine the value (the "Worth") of what they are receiving in the exchange (the "It") and make a payment for it (the "Pay"), I must state that clearly and with consistency. With time and practice, I've become adept at asking my customer to pay what it's worth, and at sharing what I mean: *You get to determine a fair value for the product/service you're receiving, and you get to communicate that worth through the price you pay.*

Share Social Responsibility

As I continue to practice employing Pay What It's Worth, what I've found to be most valuable about the system is how it supports me in clarifying: my brand and how I express it; who I serve and how to serve them best; and how I value my offerings, as well as myself and others in an exchange. Unbeknownst to me when I began my crazy pricing adventure, Pay What It's Worth would also reveal itself as a tool for discovering my own innate worth. For in order to thrive without setting prices, I had to clear my own internal energy leaks. I had to see and take action to address the ways in which I was inflating and deflating my perceived value, my goodness, and my deservedness. Consistently, whether I was conscious of them or not, my self-worth issues were affecting my business transactions, and it was only when I started to use Pay What It's Worth that I was pushed to face the limitations I was creating in my exchanges with others. In essence, Pay What It's Worth forced me to mind my own business and get real on where my responsibility lay in my relationships and exchanges. It highlighted to me this truth: it is a delicate business being generous in a way that is nourishing and sustaining. It requires giving with an open heart, while also protecting this openness from those (including yourself) who will mistake it as an opportunity to overstep boundaries. Generosity is a balancing act, and finding this equilibrium is the key to the sustainability in any pricing model, in any exchange, in any relationship. A thriving relationship needs a current of giving and receiving, co-created and co-managed between the participants. When you create a pricing system that shares this social responsibility, you have the potential to shape a business exchange that is truly nourishing for all.

A System to Uniquely Meet Your Business Needs

I've divided this book in three parts: *Understanding*, *Action*, and *The Space Between*. In *Understanding*, we'll explore the foundations of Pay What It's Worth; in *Action*, we'll apply this understanding; and in *The Space Between* we'll explore the questions that arise as you move between these two states. I've structured the book in this way to support you as you think and feel your way through creating your own design for a Pay What It's Worth system. Complex systems, such as your system for not setting prices, cannot be created overnight. They are created incrementally, layer-by-layer, step-by-step, with each iteration coming together to deliver a better whole. To begin your design, you do not need to know your solution; you simply need to be open to it existing. Beautiful systems are naturally iterative and empathetic. They grow with you and through you. As you learn, they improve. Applying design thinking to your Pay What It's Worth system will ensure you bring together what is desirable from a humanistic point of view with what is scientifically and economically viable. Through developing a better understanding of your customer needs and your own, you'll begin to recognize patterns in your information and intuit how you can best design your system to better meet these needs. With this understanding, you'll be able to apply the appropriate design tools to your system and conduct effective tests to validate their value. With this focus and interplay between understanding and action, you'll explore not setting prices with a balance of analytical thinking and intuitive knowledge; using empathy, creativity, and rationality to understand and build your system. As you play with your Pay What It's Worth system it will transform your thinking, providing you with knowledge that will sustain you—and interrupt you.

UNDERSTANDING

CHAPTER 1

The Foundations

My Truth:
Exploring the Heart of Value

It would be convenient to think my own journey with Pay What It's Worth began when I was shaping my business—but the reality is, I started on this adventure far earlier. My education, experiences, and environment were all integral to my decision to take this journey. They formed the foundation of my relationship with money, and my recognition of it as a tool for empowerment.

Business was a fundamental part of my life growing up. My father is a real estate entrepreneur and very much a traditional businessman who thinks of profit first. For him, a day is worthwhile and joyful when he makes money. As a kid, I discovered business was a powerful tool to connect with him, and to build our relationship. We would spend time together talking about his business and the business world at large. I found satisfaction and love in connecting with him this way, and in supporting him however I could, that, as odd as it may sound, business became one of my favourite tools for exchanging love. This early belief stayed with me. No matter what the rest of the world thought and taught, I knew the truth. Business is about relationships—it is about exchanging value and it is about service. It is in my nature to be loving and generous, and business became a natural tool for me to express this.

At a very early age, I also had my first lessons in understanding my external value, and my first experiences of providing a service and of being fairly paid for it. At the age of two, I was employed as a model and I received my first paycheque. I continued to work steadily as a child and to learn about the intrinsic value of doing my best work, and the external value of being paid for it. Later, when I was fresh out of undergraduate business school, I participated in my first Pay What It's Worth experience, though only years later did I realize that was what it was. I was a marketing associate, and one of my roles was doing the accounting administration for our department. Each month I would process the blank invoices of our graphic designer. My manager would determine the price on the invoice and how much our designer would receive for the project(s) he'd worked on. Their relationship's foundations were shaped by trust—he trusted her to fairly value his work, and she trusted him to skillfully and consistently deliver work she valued. There was an ease and fluidity to their relationship that unknowingly stayed with me. When I shaped my own design business this experience helped me feel confident that nurturing my relationships would continue to bring wealth into my world.

Does this truly answer why I came to question setting prices and why I was willing to risk my business health (and my personal wealth) to explore an alternative? I'd say, no, not really. The truth is there was something deeper, more unconscious, driving my decision... I was in pain, and I was looking to relieve it and heal myself, using business as a tool. Extremely sensitive to money being misused, especially to gain power over another, I was hurt by and rebelling against the scarcity mindset and fear-based messaging I saw all around me. I objectively live in abundance, and yet I had learned to believe in—and invest in—scarcity. As my colleague Ebele Mogo wrote, "a language and logic of fear and scarcity around money and finances" (personal communication, July 13, 2014) pervaded my world. With my newly forming business relationships, I could choose differently—and create things differently. Not setting prices was my way of critiquing my experience in a scarcity-focused economy, by creating a different relationship with money and with exchanging it than I had known previously. It was my money pain that led me to question my scarcity mindset and to feel I could trust people (and myself) to be fair in their giving. I needed to believe there was a different perspective on money, and of others, that I could grow wealthy with.

With these foundations of belief, thought, and experience I found myself, as a fledgling business owner, open enough to question that there might be a different (and more values-aligned) pricing method for me, one that felt more focused on the mutual creation of value. In early 2009, when my business was in its infancy, I found myself exploring pricing strategies. While on vacation, sitting in a hammock overlooking the Nicaraguan jungle and the Pacific Ocean, I was deeply engaged in the book *Secrets of the Wealthy Mind* when I encountered the question—What if your customer set the price?[3] I found myself deeply connecting to author Philip Dignan's (2007) words, and when he suggested there may be a more values-based and value-focused way of exchanging goods and services, my mind was blown (pp. 69-71). I was fascinated, intrigued. Dignan (2007, pp. 69-71) suggested I could thrive through allowing the unique needs and experiences of my customers to determine the value, and thus the price, of my offerings... *What if?* It had never occurred to me that someone other than the seller would establish value, and set prices, in a business exchange. I had never questioned setting prices before. I had always just assumed it was what businesses did, and for good reason. But when I began to consider the possibility of not setting them, it felt like a long slow fall down a rabbit hole. What would it really mean to give that power to my customer? How would that change our business exchange? How would it change the way I ran my business? Was I limiting the value I could receive by setting a price for it? The questions kept coming. Why not stop superimposing my determination of value based on arbitrary, artificial and dated economic applications? Why not instead allow my customers to collaborate with me in determining the value of my product? These questions provoked me and excited me, and I knew I needed to explore them more. And so, I found myself making the decision to experiment with this new system, and to shape it so that it reflected my own personal and business values.

I figured if not setting prices did not work, it simply did not work; at worst, I would lose money, and at best, I would gain first-hand experience and knowledge into why setting prices was necessary. Having just begun my communication design business, I had only conducted a single transaction with a client and in it, I had set the price of my service (in this instance, website design and development) based upon my understanding of the project scope and the value of my contribution, and the customer paid this price in two installments, as a deposit and final payment. What I noticed from this experience (as well as previous work experiences) was how I consistently provided excellent service that over-delivered on my customer's expectations; and what most influenced the quality of my work was not what I was being paid for it, but rather the relationship I had with the work and the person I was working with. My work and my standards for its quality were intrinsically set. I had to do my best; anything less compromised my integrity. I saw, however, that the value another placed on my work was not set in the same way, and I saw possibility in that. I saw the possibility of an individual deciding how to value my work, and I saw the possibility of allowing that value to freely grow over time. I also noticed how I valued pricing my offerings in a fair and accessible way. As a customer, I actively value great quality at a fair price, and as a business owner, it felt important to offer the same. With this growing understanding of my own behaviour and intentions, I opened myself up even more to exploring the untraditional and slightly frightening new option taking shape before me.

Entertaining these new ideas also caused me to question the techniques by which I had learned to set prices, and wonder if they were fully reflecting the value my business was providing and my customers were receiving. I considered a traditional value pricing method where I, as the business, determined and set the value the customer was receiving, and priced accordingly. Upon reflection, this model felt leading and limiting. By stating a price, I was telling the customer how to value my offering, and, in turn, I was putting limits on this value. Similarly, if I decided to price based upon the market and how I felt my product compared with it, what value was I limiting there? If I believed my work was my art, an offering wholly unique, I needed a pricing approach that would take this into account. How could I best ensure I wasn't overpricing and/or underpricing my unique offering? What was the best way to find my pricing equilibrium and provide my product at the right price maximizing my demand? Was there a way to price that took into account market prices, the customer's ability to pay, the seller's perception of value, AND the customer's perception of value? What else was relevant to pricing that I wasn't yet seeing? These questions held enough weight that, despite my fear and insecurity towards not setting prices, I decided to set down on the seemingly crazy path of doing it.

Understanding the Current of Exchange

To truly get Pay What It's Worth pricing requires being open to one simple and complex truth: there is a current of exchange that exists all around us, connecting us. You give. Others receive. Others give. You receive. Over and over we cycle together. This current, like a river, has ebbs and flows. Have you ever noticed how there are periods of your life where you are giving more? Giving less? Spending more? Spending less? Creating more? Creating less? Being aware of this natural current, its rise and fall, wax and wane, is important in managing your responses to and interactions with it. Noticing its patterns will help you to feel more abundant and less fearful about your money and finances in those times when you have less. This understanding, that what you give will be returned to you, will make you more open to risks, more generous, and more aware that you will never run out of things to give—or to receive.

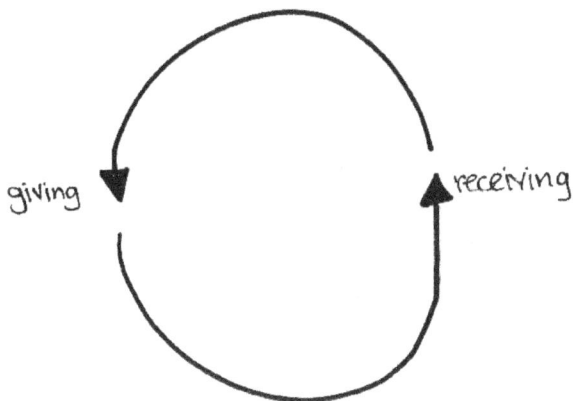

Figure 1. The current of exchange (own diagram).

This current of exchange includes not just money and resources, but exchanges of more ephemeral things, like trust. Naturally and without thought, we trust each other to act with integrity and to exchange fairly. When you cross the street at a stoplight, you may look both ways, but ultimately you trust the drivers around you not to hit you. As they trust you not to dart out into traffic. This is an example of an exchange, a mutual acknowledgement of each other's integrity.

In fact, this current of exchange underlies what it means to be human. Before I go any further, be forewarned: in the next couple paragraphs I am going to talk about nature and the deeper patterns of creation. I am also going to be talking about energy, and this word can hold a charge for some. It may feel too ungrounded for you or perhaps too spiritual, and you may feel it has no business here. If you'd like to skip ahead, I invite you to jump to the bottom of page 29, where we explore the current of exchange using Game Theory.

Still with me? Science is highly spiritual. Consider this, science is the physical exploration of nature and the deeper patterns of creation. When we speak of God, of the Universe, of Source, we are also speaking of these complex systems of nature; only in this (spiritual) context, we are really speaking about our connection to it. Whether it is the observation and study of those natural systems, and/or the practice of consciously connecting with them, we're still talking about the same, unified thing: the larger interdependent system we observe all around us. The Laws of Physics state that in this interdependent system, energy can be converted in form but it cannot be destroyed, nor created. Humans are also made of energy and obey the same law: whatever energy we put into the world must be returned to us.

One of the most visible ways we exchange energy is through an organized system we have come to call various things, including commerce, the economy, the market, and business. These economic exchanges are a vital tool for us to exchange our energy—in the forms of money, time, talent, and resources—in order to receive what we need. Money was originally created for this purpose, to act as a visible representation of our energy and its ability to be exchanged—it's called currency for a good reason. Next time you exchange a $20 bill in your wallet for a delicious meal in your belly, observe how you are exchanging your energy, in the form of the $20 bill, for the energy of another person(s), in the form of the meal created and served. To operate in our material world and prosper, you need to exchange your energy, in business exchanges and otherwise, using money and other tools. What's interesting is while you can't choose to create more energy for yourself (as energy can't be created nor destroyed); you can choose *how* you exchange your energy. The exchanges of energy you choose to participate in shape your personal current of exchange. *How* you choose to exchange affects the quality and quantity of your energy. *How* you choose to play with and change your energy affects your return. You 'grow' in wealth through learning how to exchange your energy more wisely.

Another useful theory to explore the current of exchange is Neumann and Morgenstern's (1944) Game Theory[4]—a topic popularized by the movie,

A Beautiful Mind.[5] This mathematical, economical, and psychological theory explores social interactions and strategic decision-making. It divides social interactions into two types of exchanges: 'zero-sum,' and 'non-zero-sum.' In zero-sum exchanges, one person wins and the other person(s) loses. In non-zero-sum exchanges, both parties benefit equally from the interaction. Game Theory finds behaving cooperatively and creating non-zero-sum exchanges is the most optimal way to play humanity's 'social game.' As Robert Wright (2009, p. 200) wrote, "Human existence abounds in self-serving reasons to start thinking less selfishly..."[6] Business itself offers reasons for acting in non-zero-sum ways. In its simplest sense, this behaviour encourages your customer to return for another exchange [read: repeat business]. So why do we see so many examples of zero-sum exchanges? We see them because we, as a collective and as individuals, have agreed to support them, based upon our outdated and ungrounded economic assumptions of scarcity. Our collective culture of scarcity has taught us to believe that as individuals, when it comes to money and finances, we need to invest in zero-sum language, logic, and action in order to survive and prosper. As we continue to "buy into" these false ideas, the businesses that promote and support them continue to exist and grow. What's interesting is, by questioning these scarcity and fear-based assumptions and their corresponding cultural messages, each of us has the ability to consciously shift this collective investment in zero-sum exchanges. Simply by becoming aware of your current of exchange, and exploring the optimal way to use it, you're creating social change.

Exploring Our Money Shadow

Money is a symbol of two basic principles underlying every process in the physical world: the principle of value, and the principle of giving and receiving. Whether it is our money, our labour, our commitment, or our care—we estimate the value of something by what we are willing to give for it and receive from it. This respect and attention we give to what we value, and how we value it, is a reflection of our self-worth. The lack of respect we give to the things that matter to us—including our bodies and the worth of our labour— is also a reflection of our self-worth. This unconscious lack of respect is our shadow energy around money and self-worth, and commonly manifests itself as the emotions of fear and greed, which are closely tied to our modern relationship with money and wealth. The corruption, materialism, and consumerism of modern society, and the widely disproportionate difference in wealth between the people at the top of the income ladder and the rest of society are all manifestations of our collective money shadow.

Unaware of our personal shadow energy, we have "bought into" the idea that if we can afford an item, it must measure and reflect the inherent value we hold— and if another cannot, they must be worth less and hold less value than we do. Disconnected from our own and others' true sense of worth, we are losing our intuitive sense of how much to give for the value we receive. Instead, we are building ourselves up with material accumulations, as though they alone are a reflection of our worth and deservedness. What our money shadow does not recognize is that money is only one type of currency, one type of wealth, and it is not a true measure of our self-worth. Perceiving money as the only and/or most important measure of wealth and self-worth can only leave us feeling unsatisfied. There will always be someone with more money, and thus there will always be someone for us to feel less than. While several psychological studies have revealed that although material security definitely increases our happiness, beyond a certain income level this correlation between income and happiness drops significantly. One reason for this is that a major ingredient of happiness is a sense of sufficiency—of having enough. In a culture where we are trained to consume and to compete and compare, many of us have lost the ability to recognize this feeling of satisfaction. We find ourselves feeling we do not have enough, that we are in lack, and these feelings further trigger our shadow emotions of fear and greed. We find ourselves feeling that we are not enough.

While we may not objectively live in poverty, in essence, our culture lives with a poverty consciousness. Attached to material goods as a symbol of our self-worth, we are now better equipped to feel in lack—to feel we do not have enough and are not enough—than to feel satisfied. This lack of satisfaction, this poverty consciousness, is extremely painful and often manifests in mental habits like criticism, judgment, envy, and anger. Unaware of the pain we are in, and unable to recognize a feeling of satisfaction within our self, we unconsciously invest in scarcity—we acquire for the sake of having more and more, further losing our ability to access our inner feeling of "enough." Lost in our greed, we endlessly chase the ever-receding prize that is our happiness.

It is not easy to feel whole and satisfied in a collective culture that sells you on your insufficiency. It requires cultivating a conscious awareness of how you behave and how you think. It involves actively looking at your attitudes and imbalances around money, authority, and health. There is a balance to be found between greed and generosity, between trusting in abundance and buying into scarcity. A healthy relationship with physical wealth can be cultivated within you.

Rethinking Money

Paradoxically, while money today is often used as a tool to divide, it was originally intended as a tool to unite. No society was completely self-sustaining and humans created money so they could interact with other groups. It became a common language everyone could understand. It qualified a fair exchange of one person's time, effort, and resources for that of another. Money created a more fluid means for exchanging the value we each offer as individuals. Money, fundamentally, is a means for improving the material quality of life for everyone. It is a tool of exchange and it's an agreement we all share—we're all striving for survival and security. At its core, money is something we can all agree on.

At the same time, money is also an idea, and like any concept, it holds no power other than that which you assign it. You decide how powerful money is in your world—what it means, what you need from it, and what you'll do for it. Spiritually, physically, mentally, and emotionally, money's meaning is what you give it. That's why you have different ideas about money, value, and worth than I do. Your relationship with money is yours to define. However, should you choose to abuse this relationship and misuse your power, it costs you (and the collective) in a larger and longer sense. Our money (and the economy it represents) becomes less sustainable when we are ignorant and /or irresponsible to its value and intention. Our global economy of debt and our collective environment in decline are reflections of this reality. Our collective relationship with money and value is off-balance. It lacks integrity.

Money can only function as a sustainable resource stabilizing the economy when we share an understanding of the fair value of the different elements of productivity. Our economy requires a balance of the resources that comprise the product, the labour that creates it, and the creative strategy that develops and generates it. Fair exchanges of energy and value are necessary for money to function sustainably. This fact is important to consider as you explore Pay What It's Worth: The more skillfully you engage with money and create a collective understanding of fair value—both as a customer and creator—the more you will grow (y) our economy. Money is an agreement between us all, and to use your money regeneratively, you need to be conscious of how you use (and misuse) this agreement.

It's important to acknowledge, however, that to consciously act from a place of integrity is not always a simple or easy task, AND it can be especially difficult when you're dealing with money and finances. To truly co-create mutual fulfillment, you must first be in touch with how you feel and what you need, and that's not always easy. Then, you must be clear in communicating this information to others. And that's not easy either. Most of us have grown up hearing a common message that there is not enough (we live with collective global debt), that it is not fair (the rich get richer, the poor get poorer), and that it is just the way it is (there is overwhelming apathy towards global economic reform). We've learned a poverty consciousness around money; a fear of being without and a fear of our basic needs not being met. This mindset is so deeply ingrained that most of us don't notice it—it feels normal, which makes it very easy for us to engage with it, communicate it, and project it onto others. When you're coming from this scarcity perspective, you might assume you don't have enough money and/or I don't; and/or you might assume you need to control people and how they share their money. You might feel people are neither fair nor generous with their resources naturally. In these moments, you're not trusting the integrity of others, and you're not trusting your own integrity. As a society, we share a fear that if we aren't proactive enough in meeting our needs, we won't survive. Buying into our fear of missing out, we feel inclined to grab as much as we can whenever it becomes available. These fears manifest in our culture as greed, as wanting more than our fair share, as indulgence, and as attachment. In our business culture, this scarcity perspective is seen as especially valuable, and perhaps even necessary. This poverty mindset, this connection between money and exploitation, is so prevalent you may not even notice yourself propagating it.

We all have money pain, and it can come out in both conscious and unconscious ways. Your mindset on, and approach to, money (or any *thing*) is communicated each time you exchange it. When you exchange a *thing*, your intentions, both conscious and not, are communicated by your language and your logic, and your subsequent actions. Even your expression at the moment of exchange can signify your deeper emotions. Therefore, it's of immense benefit to you and your business to be mindful of your varying feelings, thoughts, and actions around money. Some unconscious money approaches you might find yourself employing are: 'taking'—where you drain another person in fear of losing what you've worked so hard for; 'over-giving'—where you hold yourself unworthy and allow others to take advantage of you; 'fearing money'—where you place money outside of your conscious self and you reject it in some way; 'dominating money'—where you feel you alone have generated what you've earned, and you control the flow of money; and 'having too much'—where you feel you have more money than you will ever need and you lack respect for it. While each of these unconscious approaches looks and feels different, from not sharing your gifts to undervaluing your relationships, they ultimately are a misuse of your power, and produce results misaligned with your integrity. They will not serve you or the person you are exchanging with. A conscious approach to money, however, benefits you, and everyone you do business with. It's simple and natural and it's about creating non-zero-sum exchanges. This can feel like approaching money from a perspective of 'giving', where you enter an exchange focused not on what you can get but what you can give. More neutral than 'giving' is the perspective of 'matching', where you enter an exchange focused on what is fair and balanced. In both instances, you receive what you give, and your current of exchange is amplified. As we continue to explore Pay What It's Worth pricing I'm applying the intention of 'matching' and/or 'giving' in my language and logic around money to ensure I'm supporting you in consciously creating the results you desire. In increasing your awareness around money and the meaning you place on it, you're consciously evolving your relationship with it and with yourself. In learning to hold yourself up mentally with more integrity, you're increasing your ability to consistently create non-zero-sum exchanges and to build an effective Pay What It's Worth system.

The Importance of Integrity

Figure 2. Integrity is only a Venn diagram away (own drawing).

Your integrity requires you to be authentic while also being responsible to yourself, and others. You experience your integral self when you're in a natural state of generosity, trusting you can act from a place of abundance and honesty. In her book, *The Nature of Investing*, Katherine Collins (2014, p.13) theorizes that once in this integral space, you instinctively invest in connection, exchange, and mutual benefit.[7] By doing so, you contribute to your own wealth, and that of your stakeholders. Collins, using the context of investing, proves what Game Theory explores—that it simply makes dollars and sense to invest in your own wealth, and that of the collective. To build a Pay What It's Worth pricing system that works, you need to connect with your integrity, and that of your customer.

Your integrity is founded upon four conscious intentions that you must be dedicated to inspiring, evolving, and implementing. The first of these intentions is **empathy**. Your integrity is contingent upon your focused consideration of your customers and the experience they are receiving. Step into their shoes and see what you are providing from the perspective of their needs, their desires, and their expectations. What experience is your business creating? How does working with your business make them feel? These components are, in essence, your brand. The experience your business creates stays with your customers. They remember it. You *brand* them with it. The way you brand people is your most powerful tool for communicating your integrity.

Trust is the second intention in building the foundations of your integrity. What do you bring to a relationship that produces trust? Do you trust yourself?

If you don't trust yourself, you cannot truly give to others; your actions will be motivated by other deep-seeded fears and insecurities. Knowing how you trust and what you need in a relationship, however, lets you completely commit yourself. Trusting people is one of the most difficult challenges in life since there is always the fear of getting hurt. Understanding your ability to trust and be trusted helps you remain committed to others. Building trust in your business, however, can't be one-sided. It must be based not only on what you do, but also on what your customers do. As Dale Carnegie (1981, p. 210) said, "Give the other person a fine reputation to live up to."[8] You get to create opportunities for your customer to show their love and integrity and for you to show yours. You have the powerful opportunity to co-create the currency of exchange, aligning and inventing how generously you value and benefit each other. In doing your best on behalf of your customer, and trusting that your customer is doing their best on behalf of you, you will create something truly lasting and valuable—an economy of integrity.

The third intention in building the foundations of your integrity is **worth**. Creating products and/or services that offer lasting value for your customers is necessary to build the foundations of integrity in your business. If you are creating authentic value, you are not selling a commodity: you are creating something truly distinctive, something completely unique. It's important that you believe this AND communicate it. Do not ask people to fairly value something you are not fairly valuing yourself. What people value, they will pay for. But you may need to help them to do so fairly. You can do this by focusing on your customers and the unique value you create for them. Then your business becomes a mini-monopoly where your customers are willing to pay for the brand they trust. After all, you are the only *you*.

The last required intention in molding the foundations of integrity is that of **mindful action**. In every decision you make, nurturing and protecting your integrity is necessary to build systems with integrity in your business and life. It's your responsibility to invest in abundance as consistently and consciously as you can. One of the most vital contributions you can make to build an integrity-based world is to dedicate time to consistently work on aligning your actions mindfully, with introspection and deliberation. Your integrity is your most valuable wealth creation tool and it takes daily practice to consistently make choices that support its growth.

What's exciting and challenging about using—and growing—the Pay What It's Worth pricing approach is how necessary it is to continuously connect with and reinforce your integrity. You need to be aware of your intentions and your actions, and if they're aligning to create the results you desire. While your success is contingent on your talent, effort, and creativity, it first and foremost requires your willingness to receive. You need to be receptive to your customer, and interact with them in realistic ways without putting yourself in jeopardy. Through these smart business practices and mindfulness practices, you'll find yourself healing your money stuff, better realizing your worth, and expanding the wealth of your business. It is within these limitless conditions that you'll find a solid and sustainable system for consciously creating the abundance you desire.

To achieve this, you need to create a system that will support you in being idealistic and authentic in your pricing and in your service. Being realistic about your needs will guide you in building a sustainable context for your business – one that is beneficial to the community as well as yourself. This framework will enable you to remain focused on your work and your performance, and remove the need for judgment calls and/or extraneous tasks. Your system will also allow you to be idealistic, in your service and in your pricing, by authentically supporting it. In *The Economics of Integrity*, Anna Bernasek (2010, pp. 142-145) identifies three necessary ingredients to ensure *any* system (natural or man-made) has integrity and is sustainable. These three ingredients are:

DISCLOSURE

The open sharing of information

NORMS

Clear and well-founded boundaries

ACCOUNTABILITY

Responsibility for choices and actions[9]

Disclosure in a system is necessary as sharing information leaves the truth out in the open and allows each person to make his or her own informed decisions about the exchange. Norms are critical as rules and boundaries in a system help to inhibit our desire to exploit the trust of others, and they create a simple framework for how we are expected to behave. Accountability establishes responsibility and awareness that there are consequences for acting poorly. In a sense, these three conditions are what give our integrity structure. They support you in caring for yourself by being present to your relationships, and realistic in them. In the coming pages, we'll explore strategies for building business systems of integrity, through the creation of and investment in disclosure, norms, and accountability. We'll also explore how these conditions are the same ones needed to build all sustainable relationships—in business and otherwise. Together, we will learn how we can empower ourselves to create and invest in relationships, economies, and other systems where all stakeholders grow wealthy together.

CHAPTER 2

Building Your System

My Truth:
Minding My Business (Systems)

As someone who's an idealist at heart, I need to be discerning to compensate for the natural naiveté of my character. With equal care, I've learned to nurture these seemingly opposing characteristics, allowing me to remain open to ideas and people, while staying realistic to the potential of being drained, disappointed, and/or trapped by them. Through practice, discernment has become one of my favourite tools for determining what is working and what is not in my life and business. It empowers me to make changes, and to know there's always something I can do to improve my situation. Becoming more skilled at noticing the subtle distinctions between things, people, and experiences, I've found myself better able to notice what isn't working for me. Unconvering this information, my naiveté inspires confidence that I can solve the problem, and my discernment supports me in actually doing so. In action, this dance looks like me striving to know and become aware of what my capacities are, and how they can be best utilized and applied. In a way, I see my life as a system, and I am the creator, continuously designing a better version.

When I began my experiment with not setting prices, I discerned that it would be far too easy (and naive) of me, should I find my product being undervalued, to immediately blame the customer and their actions and hold them wholly accountable for the results. While the customer and their "stuff" would help create the situation, I also needed to recognize that my "stuff" would contribute. What I mean by "stuff" is, we all have topics and situations that can unconsciously trigger feelings of fear and lack, and these triggers, when not responsibly managed, can cause us to co-create zero-sum exchanges. Holding myself accountable to this reality, I concluded that I needed to think of my system for not setting prices in the same way I thought about my life, as a system with the potential to constantly be improved. Any problems I identified were holes in my system in need of repair. For it was the system (and me as its creator) giving space for others to behave in unfavourable ways. Feeling I could blame the customer would only foster fear-based thoughts of victimization, and cloud my view of what was *wholly* going on. I was as responsible for creating a situation where my work could be under-valued, as my customer was for undervaluing it.

This shared responsibility seems to be the heart of Pay What It's Worth. For whenever I allowed the inevitable emotion that accompanies unfavourable exchanges to pass, these experiences always proved to be powerful sources of information for growing my pricing system and my relationships. They consistently helped me to identify weaknesses in my system and address them. Working to understand the problem clearly, beyond the emotion of it, highlighted the value of creating and constantly reinforcing a strong system for not setting prices. The system maximized my potential of being of service and my client's potential of being generous with me, by creating appropriate boundaries and limits for us to work within. Similarly, it was the system that shaped our shared responsibility, and the fluidity of our business relationship and the establishment of trust between us. Through it, my business saved time, money, and energy by not trying to find the "optimal" price point that maximized the accessibility of my product, its demand, and my return. Instead, I allowed my customer to show me what the demand was for my product(s), where my product's optimal price was, and how it fluctuated over time and with the person who is valuing it. This trust and shared responsibility fed our relationship and resulted in delighted customers, repeat and frequent business, as well as generous word-of-mouth, as the customer was consistently happy with the product, their experience, and the price paid for it. My right customer was drawn to my brand's quality and qualities, its more values-based pricing approach, and its focus on exchanging mutual value. Pay What It's Worth emerged for me as a powerful un-marketing practice, deflecting my un-ideal customer, one who was not seeking mutually beneficial exchanges and/or was not confident enough to explore their sense of value.

On the topic of responsibility, my Pay What It's Worth system also made it very clear to me that despite our cultural messages, I am never asking the customer to determine *my* worth. No one is looking to buy my worth—they want my product. My worth cannot be measured, earned, nor sold anyway; but my product certainly can be. It is the object of exchange—as is our shared perception of it. To illustrate what I mean about our shared perception, ask yourself: Is the value of the Empire State Building high because the value of rent is high, or vice versa, is the value of rent high because the building is highly valued? Does your answer change if I asked you to substitute *what* you are valuing? For example, is the value of a cow high because the value of calves and milk is high, or vice versa, is the value of milk and calves high because cows are highly valued? In altering *what* you are valuing, did your answer change? I share this analogy with you (created by an American business professor whose name I wish I knew) to highlight that your willingness to pay is fluid, and not set. How you and I value things and what we are willing to pay depends on how we perceive the thing we're valuing. Pricing and prices are one such tool we use to shape perception. Believing I did not need to state the value of my product in order for the customer to recognize it, and coming to understand I wasn't selling my worth, I saw how critical it was for me to effectively represent my brand and my product's worth, and to support others' generous perception of it. To truly do that, I had to understand the value of the product I was offering and I had to communicate this value in other subtler (non-price-specific) ways in order to thrive. When I wasn't balanced in my communication, and misrepresented the value of my offering, my customer noticed (consciously or not) and mirrored it back to me through their behaviour and actions. My feelings—and holding my work and myself in high accord—over and over affected how my customer valued my product. To ensure I was giving my work the credit it deserved, I got more skilled at watching my feelings and my beliefs, as well as my methods, when I exchanged my products with others. My inevitable moments of fear and of lack supported me in checking in with myself—about the value I was actually adding to my business relationships, and how my fearful actions were reducing it. As I continued to increase my awareness around my work and its value, I noticed my wealth increased and I found my pricing system running more smoothly. Learning to value myself and my products more authentically and wholly, my customer was naturally placing a higher value on them too. It seemed my discernment and my naiveté had supported me in successfully shaping a system for pricing that naturally supported my current of exchange.

Your Constraint to Not Setting Prices

In their Management Science study, Isaac, Lightle, and Norton (2010) of Florida State University's Economics Department found that a business can return potentially higher profits (in comparison to setting prices) if the brand experience is:

SMALL

EXCLUSIVE

INTIMATE

LOYALTY BUILDING

PERSONAL[10]

Their study found businesses that are relationship- and experienced-focused, that create small, exclusive, intimate, loyalty-building and personal relationships with their customers, have the potential to thrive with not setting prices. It's wise and lucrative for these types of businesses to not set prices as they're creating business conditions where their stakeholders are connected to the value they are receiving and giving.

Another interesting study, this one by UC San Diego Rady School of Management and Disney Research (Gneezy, Gneezy, Nelson, & Brown, 2010), explored the viability of connecting not setting prices with charitable giving.[11] Conducting their experiment at a popular rollercoaster, they asked riders to determine the price of their post-rollercoaster action photos. Applying different conditions to *what* the customer was valuing—from just the photo to the photo and a donation to a specific charity—they found not setting prices to be a viable pricing strategy and social responsibility strategy for companies—when the customer's willingness to give was stimulated. They found that the more a customer feels connected to what they are giving to—and that they have a choice in what and how much they're giving—the more willing they are to give. The study's findings showed that when a buyer knows their money will benefit something or someone specific—such as a charity, the creator, or a small business and its owner and staff—they feel a more tangible and human connection to the product and the exchange relationship. As a result, they are more open to giving, and to giving generously. Interestingly, the study concluded creating these types of opportunities for "shared social responsibility" may provide the critical

sustainability component that is often lacking in current
social responsibility strategies.

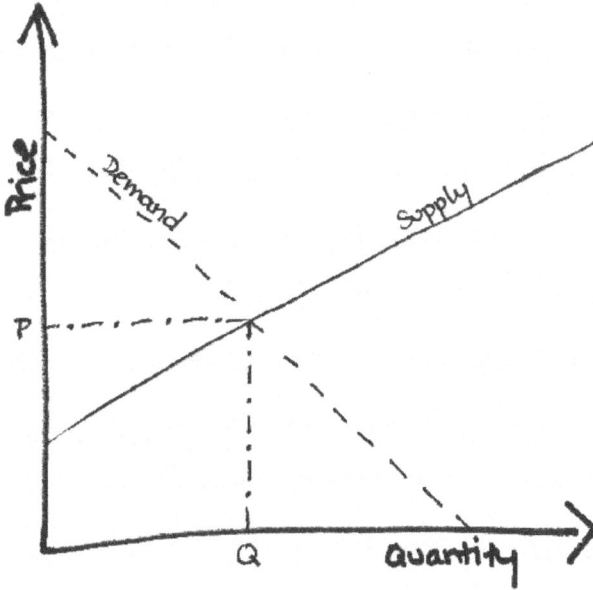

Figure 3. The theory of supply and demand
(own drawing).

From a purely economic viewpoint, the economic
theory of supply and demand makes similar conclusions about the viability of not setting prices. The theory
assumes the quantity demanded falls as the price of a
good rises, and conversely the quantity supplied rises
as the price increases. According to this theory, if you
supply your good at the level of demand, i.e., your
customer sets the price and the quantity purchased,

two things will happen: you will maximize your return potential rather than limit it; and you will shift the traditional supply curve based upon scarcity to one based upon abundance. In allowing people to pay their own price, according to the theory, you are creating a movement that allows you to extract the marginal value of each buyer. Some will pay more and some will pay less. Some will buy more and pay less; while some will pay more and buy less. According to economic science, it makes logical sense to consider not setting prices.

However, the business studies we previously explored show there is more to the story. Pricing is more than just a logic-based science; it is also an emotion-based art. Taking into account action as well as theory, shows a more complete truth than theory alone. To thrive not setting prices, your business must stimulate generosity. It must invest in and foster our innate desire for mutual benefit, exchange, and connection. It must co-create an integrity-filled current of exchange. Those exchanging with your business need to connect with its purpose and values for them to respond in kind. To facilitate this, marketing thought-leader Simon Sinek (2009, p. 80) suggests in *Start With Why* that "The goal is not to do business with everyone who needs what you have, the goal is to do business with people who believe what you believe."[12] To assess if Pay What It's Worth is a fit for you, start by considering these questions: What is your business supporting? Does small, exclusive, intimate, loyalty building, and personal describe your business conditions and goals? If your business is not inherently creating an exchange experience that promotes generosity, this is a major impediment to building a healthy Pay What It's Worth system.

Building a System that Lasts

Building a sustainable system for exchanging your business offerings with others—and not setting prices—is contingent upon you creating a sense of connection with your customer. You must stimulate generosity with the pricing system you build. To begin building these generous foundations requires you to recognize and explore two immutable truths:

1. What you put into your system for not setting prices is what you get out of it.

   i) This speaks to your intentions. It really matters *why* you are choosing this type of pricing method. Whether you are aware of your initial motivations or not, they will inevitably colour your communications and actions, and ultimately affect your results. As such, it is important to be introspective and understand the rationale behind your decisions, incentives, motives, and goals.

   ii) The next step is to be confident in your decision to not set prices and to communicate this sense of abundance to your customers.

   iii) Once you have established a relationship with a customer based on Pay What It's Worth, the exchange will succeed only if you treat your relationships with care. They are the foundation of your system.

2. How your system will work best for your business is yours to discover.

   i) In your business, you are the artist. You determine its colour, texture and intensity. Your pricing and business needs will be unique, as will the way you meet them, and the nuances and personal touches you use. Your system will become yours once it uniquely reflects your business.

ii) Your system will be as strong and resilient as you are. Through your life experiences, you have grown an awareness of your relationships with your self, with money and value, with your customers, and with your work. What makes you unique, what drives you in life, and what your goals are will reflect in your system. And as you absorb more of life's lessons, the structure of your system will grow and improve with you.

With these truths in mind, ask yourself the following questions about your intentions for not setting prices and for building a Pay What It's Worth pricing system for your business:

1) **What are you investing in?**

You are an investor. This is true for all of us. You invest in yourself and you invest in others. You do this as a citizen, as a customer, as a business owner, as a friend. Each action you take is an investment in something. You invest in your health through exercise and eating well, in your soul through creative expression and inspiration, in your family through communication and empathy, and in your business and vocation through time, energy, and money. You make these investments because they serve your needs, your communities, and your planet best. This is the natural way of investing, which supports our collective abundance, but, as previously discussed, it has been degraded by prevailing messages of scarcity and fear, particularly when it comes to financial investments. Acknowledging this, you need to explore your intention for not setting prices, beyond making a profit. An investment in building a pricing system with integrity that is sustainable and wealth-creating for all stakeholders is critical to your success. You have an opportunity to embrace integrity with every choice you make, and you can do so by considering the environment you want to participate in—either one of poverty consciousness or one of confidence and abundance—and acting accordingly. Are you confident you will invest wisely?

2) **How do you operate in relationships and in exchanges with other people?**
According to Adam Grant (2013a, p. 5), professor of management at the University of Pennsylvania's Wharton School of Business and the author of *Give and Take: A Revolutionary Approach to Success,* there are three types of people: the Taker, the Matcher, and the Giver.[13] To illustrate, when you're helping someone, do you expect a favour in return? If you answer yes and/or maybe, you may be a Taker and/or a Matcher. If you answer no, you may be a Giver. If your initial thought is about what can you *get* from an exchange, pay attention to that; your fear of exploitation may be causing you to focus on what is in it for you. As we've explored, you cannot create connection, exchange, and mutual benefit in your relationships when you act from a place of *taking,* where you create zero-sum

exchanges. Similarly, if you self-identify as a Giver, you need to pay attention to this and be sure to distinguish your generosity from your approaches to timidity, to availability, and to empathy. Grant (2013b) states these three qualities are often confused with generosity—and can hinder your (and others') growth when misused.[14] Sometimes, we give for the wrong reasons, and when we do it's not helpful for anyone. When you can accept this truth and the value of both sides—timidity and assertiveness, availability and security, and empathy and perspective taking—in your relationships, you'll find you are a Giver who grows wealthy from your actions (Grant, 2013b). Whatever way of being you identify with, understand this is an expression of your current of exchange; it speaks to how you co-create your relationships. Does your style complement what you know about Pay What It's Worth?

3) **How well do you know your business?**
A business is a complex entity, created from your knowledge and experiences. The unique conditions of your business will guide your success with not setting prices. Before you start, ask yourself: How does my business operate best? What is my brand? Who do I best serve? What about my business experience makes me unique? These are the elements that differentiate and ignite your system.

Before you begin building your Pay What It's Worth system, it's important you find some clarity around these questions so you know you're building a system of integrity for your business and its stakeholders. The goal is for you to know how good it feels to allow your extra energy and resources to flow through you, rather than trying to hold onto them. The goal is to build trust in the concept that you are capable of acquiring what you need, and that you can share your abundance with others. Cultivating this perspective is how you create a healthy and sustainable Pay What It's Worth system.

Perceptions of Value

One major way we limit our exchanges and relationships is through relinquishing our responsibility for them. What's exciting about the Pay What It's Worth system is you have the opportunity to create emotionally responsible AND financially responsible business exchanges. Through your system for doing business, you're empowering yourself and your stakeholders to tune into their natural state of generosity, creating freedom for everyone to naturally invest in and grow the relationship. What's interesting is, when you create choice for your customer, giving them the freedom and structure to decide the value of your exchange and what to pay for it, they will consider (consciously or unconsciously) four areas of their experience. These four areas represent the different ways we, as humans, perceive anything and everything in our world, including the value of the things and people outside of ourselves. You can explore these different doors to our perception in more detail by exploring Ken Wilbur's (2007) Integral Framework, a meta-theory that allows every area of human inquiry to see itself in relation to every other field, on the same conceptual map.[15] In brief, one concept it illustrates is how you perceive the world using your Emotional Body, your Mental Body, your Physical Body, and your Spiritual Body. In a business exchange, accessing your Emotional Body, you'll consider your level of satisfaction with the exchange, and the level of satisfaction with the brand or person you're exchanging with. For example, as a customer, you may ask yourself, Am I happy with what I have received? Will the seller be happy with what I give? In this moment, you'll perceive the world with your feelings, considering how you feel, and possibly how the creator may feel. Accessing your Physical Body, you'll assess your abilities (financially and otherwise) to contribute to the exchange and the ability (financially and otherwise) of the brand or person you're exchanging with. For example, as a customer, you may ask yourself, How much do I want to contribute to this exchange? How much has the seller/their brand contributed to this exchange? In this moment, you'll perceive the world with your material resources and physical awareness. Perceiving with your Mental Body, you'll consider the market for the exchange and the brand or person you're exchanging with. For example, as a customer, you may ask yourself, How do I value what I have received based upon my knowledge and experience of the market? How does the brand value itself and its offering based upon knowledge and experience of the market? In this moment, you'll perceive the world with your logical mind. Perceiving with your Spirit, you'll consider the fairness of the exchange. For example, as a customer, you may ask yourself, Am I coming from a place of giving or matching? Is the brand? In this moment, you'll perceive the world with your values and your sense of self.

When you have a choice in what you pay, you have an opportunity to explore and express the different ways you perceive value and to connect directly with the value you're receiving. In assuming this emotional, physical, spiritual, and mental responsibility, you'll naturally connect more with the thing you're valuing, as you're acknowledging your relationship to it. When shaping your system's integrity—represented by the creation of disclosure, norms, and accountability—it's of value for you to create freedom and structure for your customers to consider and value each of these four components of their experience fairly. In doing this, they will be able to conceive more fully their values and the value of what you are providing. Support them in considering the meaning of your exchange (the satisfaction), the contributions to the exchange (the abilities provided), the environment of the exchange (the market realities), and the relationship of the exchange (the fairness). Do what you can to help your customer be considerate of, and connect to, the full value and mutual benefit of your relationship, so you can create exchanges that authentically support your customer in naturally being generous with you.

Your Economic Opportunity to Co-create

The ideology of profit-centred, self-centred, protectionist capitalism fails as a worldview to guide us through the twenty-first century. Our current economic system is not sustainable. Billionaire financier George Soros (1997, p. 45) made the same conclusion in the *Atlantic Monthly*, "Although I have made a fortune in the financial markets, I now fear that the untrammeled intensification of laissez-faire capitalism and the spread of market values into all areas of life is endangering our open and democratic society. The main enemy of the open society, I believe, is no longer the communist but the capitalist threat."[16] As Paul Hawken (2010, p. 18) wrote in *The Ecology of Commerce*, "The glories of the global industrial economy mask the fact that it is poised at a declining horizon of options and possibilities. Just as internal contradictions brought down Marxist and socialist economies, so do a different set of social and biological forces signal our own possible demise."[17] We are in need of a more mindful capitalism. We are in need of a capitalism where we are responsible to the impact of our investments and the true costs of the things we acquire. Futurist Barbara Hubbard (2015a, p. 91) surmised it best in *Conscious Evolution*, "If we do not recognize that every business, corporation, or enterprise is part of a whole system, and must take feedback from the whole system, and be accountable for its effect on the environment, we cannot continue to evolve, or even survive."[18] This responsibility to the whole system is equally important for the customers and other stakeholders of these businesses, corporations, and enterprises—as they, too, need to recognize their place in the whole system, if we are to co-create a sustainable economic system. As customers, it is critical we understand how vital we are, as no company will continue a practice or product you, the consumer, will not buy. Choosing to spend our money wisely, we can promote those companies that do business in a socially responsible way. As Hubbard (2015b, p. 101) wrote, "The goal is a sustainable, regenerative economy that supports restoration of the environment, preservation of species, and the enhancement of human creativity and community, including expanded ownership, network marketing, community-based currencies, microcredit loans, and other such innovations."[19] Reaching these economic goals requires grassroots leaders, like you.

Before any improvement can be made in the way the world operates, an idea has to be formed and someone has to imagine how that idea could change things. If you imagine a different kind of market society and a different way of valuing the world, understand you have the opportunity to create it. You have the power and ability to create your own economy and your own system for doing business. What I mean is, you have the power to create your own means for exchanging and valuing your products and services. You have the power to decide what the current of exchange feels like in your business. The type of economy and market you inhabit, as a customer and as a business, is yours to define and to choose. You have a choice in whom you do business with, and how. When building your Pay What It's Worth pricing system and communicating about it, consider what economy you want to participate in and act accordingly. Each decision you make, in business or not, is an investment in your wealth. It's your responsibility to treat this investment with care, as your relationships are the foundations of your business. In being clear in your intentions and what you value, and acting on them, you're harnessing your power and ability to create a values-driven and integrity-filled world for your business. And in allowing your values to drive your decisions, you're creating and supporting a sustainable system for valuing the world. You've co-created an economy of integrity; a wealth creation strategy comprised of investing in the long-term growth of not only your business, but all its stakeholders. In doing this, you're helping them release their fear of lack and destruction, and you're stimulating their responsibility towards generosity. Together, you, your business, and its stakeholders take on a more mature role as co-creators and mindful capitalists.

If you have a drive to change our image of the world, and our sense of identity, you'll likely identify as a member of a global subculture known as "Cultural Creative"[20] and/or "Integral Culture."[21] You transcend modern and traditional cultural values and definitions, and in not attacking nor rejecting either of these perspectives, you're able to find a space in between them, taking what works and leaving what doesn't—allowing yourself, the people around you and the planet to flourish. As self-identified Cultural Creative Barbara Hubbard (2015c, p. 67) brilliantly wrote in *Conscious Evolution,* "We are evolution becoming self-aware."[22] As a collective, our cultural purpose is to evolve our communities and our world so we are all free to fulfill our highest potential. You, like me, are here to evolve and expand our systems—in business and otherwise—so we can each reach a place where we know our purpose and live a life of meaning. As Hubbard (2015d, p. 67) wrote, "From the perspective of conscious evolution, *Homo sapiens*, in our current phase, is a transitional species. We are not viable in this state of separated consciousness with so much power. We will either evolve or become extinct."[23] And evolve we must, from passive experiencers of life into conscious participants and co-designers. By creating systems that support people in releasing themselves from fear, we're supporting others in self-actualizing. Abraham Maslow (1954) defines the "self-actualized" person as one participating in "self-rewarding work," as they've identified the core functions or life purposes behind their chosen work.[24] By supporting others in self-actualizing, and getting their needs met, you're helping yourself and others find partners to co-create with, awakening the greater genius in people everywhere. You're helping to catalyze what Maslow identifies as the "self-actualizing society," by awakening our innerpreneur and the power of our social potential. Pay What It's Worth is just one economic tool you can employ in reaching these integral goals, for it supports you in answering your call to be more, to find your life purpose, and to contribute your gifts to the evolution of the world. It pushes you to become aware of your innate worth; and it's one of the many systems we're re-designing to highlight and evolve our collective social potential.

Now that you've consciously explored your ideas around money, value, and pricing, I offer to you, in the following sections, concrete methods to sustain this awareness. Understanding the limitations and the possibilities of Pay What It's Worth, you're now ready to consider this understanding, and what the action of not setting prices can look like for your business. In the end, your success with Pay What It's Worth and your system for not setting prices will depend on your communication, and if it is connecting with your customers to create an environment of generosity and shared responsibility. In the coming pages you will learn how to apply design thinking methods to support and enhance communication and connection—and learn how to test the validity of their effectiveness. Are your business strategies and tactics effective in diffusing the right information? Are you being clear about what you do, why you do it, and how you're valuable? Your intention, in the end, is to build a system that is grounded. Money is a currency; it flows between two points and carries energy, and it needs grounding to sustain the connection. Your Pay What It's Worth system, effectively implemented, will provide this grounding.

THE SPACE BETWEEN

CHAPTER 3
Paying What It's Worth

"Price is what you pay. Value is what you get."[25]

—Warren Buffet

Here's the thing about Pay What It's Worth: on a micro level it's a pricing practice, and on a macro level it is a perspective on—and approach to—life. Desiring and creating non-zero-sum relationships and exchanges can transform our human systems. On a macro level, these systems include religion and the financial markets, and on a micro level, family structures and how we interact with one another in interpersonal relationships. The macro systems inform the micro, and the micro mirror the macro. So, truly, as families and interpersonal relationships change, so, too, will financial systems and religion. Are you ready to change though? Do you feel it's worth it and/or necessary to be responsible to the true cost of the things you desire and acquire? Do you feel the value of being more connected to and informed about the worth of things in your world? Do you really want to explore your relationship with value, while examining your own values?

Our collective culture actively promotes the value of getting things cheap. Often, we're encouraged to feel satisfied and "smart" when we can get a deal or—better yet—a steal. In the same vein, we're often taught to feel shameful and "foolish" when we pay the full price for something. These contrasting and mirroring messages train us to disconnect from the true value and cost of the things we acquire. Wholly aware of these pervading messages, I certainly won't blame you—nor shame you—for not wanting to examine what it might mean to "pay the price." It may very well not be worth it to you.

Consider, though, why is it a good thing for you to pay less than something is worth, beyond the obvious money savings? Does happiness really result when you underpay for something of value to you? Often we are so far removed from what it cost to create and deliver a product that it's hard for us to understand the true value of the thing we are buying. But when we have firsthand evidence of the love, talent, time, and energy put into something—when we feel connected and responsible to the value of it—why would it feel good and serve us to undervalue it? How do you feel when your own time, talent, energy, or love is undervalued? If you believe that you get what you give, that creating zero-sum exchanges will not benefit you in the long term, why would you not simply strive for a fair deal in your transactions—where both participants are respected and valued? Why would it not be okay to pay what it's worth?

Should you feel that paying what it's worth is, in fact, worth it to you, here are five foundational questions to consider when creating your system:

1. How Do I Get Started?

As we will explore in depth in the coming chapters, to get started building a new system, you need to first assess your current system(s) and relationships. How much integrity do they have? And in what ways are accountability, norms, and disclosure already present in them? Whether you are starting your business, growing your business, and/or simply wanting to become a more conscious customer, looking at the systems and relationships you're choosing to invest in is key. They are the foundations upon which you will build and shape your new system. How you chose to "do business" and whom you choose to "do business with" needs to support your new goal of shared responsibility and mutual benefit.

Some of your current relationships will be enhanced by your new system of exchange, and some will not. For those you feel have the potential to grow with you, what kinds of changes and communications are needed to support them in adapting and transforming to your approach? For those relationships and systems you feel cannot be enhanced by your new operating system, what kinds of changes and communications are needed to support them in transitioning and ending? Identifying where your relationships need to be transformed, ended, and enhanced will help you acquire the knowledge you need to integrate the fundamental systems of your business—marketing, finance, human resources, accounting, and operations—into your new system of exchange.

Smoothly integrating your business systems with your new system of exchange will require you to identify, strategize, and communicate what exactly your business is asking your customer to do. Without prices informing the exchange of value, some basic business questions need to be answered:

*How does our exchange work and how do I
effectively communicate this?*

*What are my needs as the seller and what role
does the customer play in meeting them?*

*What are the customer's needs and what role
as the seller do I play in meeting them?*

What is truly being exchanged and valued between us?

These questions will inevitably lead you to a larger one:

*What do I need and what am I asking for
in my business exchanges?*

Your exploration of this question will provide the foundation for your experience and your system.

Honestly assessing your needs, and how well they are being met by the current systems and relationships you invest in, will uncover the spaces where you can create more norms, accountability, and disclosure in your exchanges. These areas in need of improvement are the very places where your new system will begin to take shape.

2. How Do I Talk About Pay What It's Worth?

You will find holding the focus of the exchange—to create mutual benefit—of utmost importance when communicating about Pay What It's Worth and not setting prices. Coming from this focused space and being clear on your intentions, no matter whom you are talking to or what perspective they hold, you'll find your language and logic communicates an abundant perspective that supports the fair exchange of value and worth.

The pitfalls in consistently communicating about Pay What It's Worth with an abundant perspective are your own (completely understandable) fears around money, and how you may unconsciously react to these, when triggered by another. To counteract this, your job when talking about Pay What It's Worth (and thinking about it) is to consciously and continuously assess if you are using any fear-based language and logic. In *Chapter 2*, we explored what your fear-based language and logic around money might look like.

Abundant and non-zero-sum language and logic may involve consciously using such words and concepts as: exchange (to create a shared understanding of what you're doing), mutual benefit and shared responsibility (to create a shared understanding of the goal), worth (to create a shared understanding of what's being assessed), value (to create a shared understanding of what's being mutually exchanged), trust (to create a shared understanding of your relationship's foundations), and generosity (to create a shared understanding of the intention of your exchange).

3. Do I Need to Have a Price in Mind? What If I Have a Price in Mind?

Whether you are a buyer or a seller, you will find it is not necessary nor detrimental to have a price in mind to engage in a Pay What It's Worth exchange. You'll find your own experience in the exchange will provide you with ample opportunities to recognize and assess the value of exchange.

As a seller, should you find you have a very fixed idea about your product's value or no sense of its value, you may want to explore setting a minimum /maximum price, and/or providing a suggested price for your product. These tools will help you to explore the value of your product and its variable worth, and how you communicate it effectively. You can learn more about applying these tools in *Chapter 4*. What you may find more helpful, however, is to explore in more depth how you're perceiving and communicating your product's worth, and how you feel when your product is being fairly valued (monetarily and otherwise). Your Pay What It's Worth exchanges are an ideal practice ground for you to explore this sense of value and how to communicate it.

As a buyer, should you find you have a very fixed idea about the value of a product or no sense of its value, you may want to take some space to explore your experience of the product in more depth. In *Chapter 2,* we explored the various frames of reference we use to fairly assess value. Looking at them, is there any aspect of your buying experience that you're currently not considering and being responsible to? Should you feel you're being conscious in your role, there is absolutely no issue with you possessing a strong sense of worth or a mutable one.

When you pay what it's worth, the price you pay and the value you receive in an exchange comfortably fluctuates with each relationship. The system creates space for your unique approach to money and value. Your job, when exchanging, is simply to ensure the perspectives you hold are conscious.

4. How Can I Tell If My System Is Working?

To check the health of your system, ask yourself:

Are my needs being met?

Are my stakeholders needs being met?

*Do I feel I'm giving and receiving fair value
in my exchanges?*

If you feel your business needs are being met, it's likely your system is working well. Still, you need to check in with it regularly and be aware that places will emerge where improvement is needed. Your system is alive and growing, and to keep it functioning well, you'll need to allow its form to adapt and evolve.

If you do not feel your business needs are being met by your system, this does not categorically mean your system isn't working. Rather, likely there are holes in your system in need of repair. These very places are what you need to pay attention to, and your first step in repairing them is determining if there is an appropriate and acceptable solution to the problem they pose. Your system will grow strong from reinforcing and supporting areas where you identify weakness. Do not ignore these gaps.

To identify these holes in your system, you need to pay attention to your exchanges and objectively assess where and when you feel they aren't going well. Rather than reacting to the issues your exchanges and your customers are presenting, you have the opportunity, using your system, to respond to these issues and correct them through direct communication and an improvement of your system's boundaries. You can ensure you're responding to—rather than reacting to—your system's issues by watching your behaviour with the person you're in exchange with. You know you're reacting when you're blaming them, and/or when you're avoiding communication and/or being overly aggressive in it, and you also know you're reacting when you don't feel like adding value and/or when you're feeling overly assertive of the value you provide. Blaming, passively contributing, passively communicating, aggressively contributing, aggressively communicating—these are all signs something isn't working for you.

What happens, though, when the issue is not the system itself, but rather the person you are exchanging with, such as your customer? This situation requires careful analysis. Likely, there is something about your system that has helped create the unfavourable situation, and it is your responsibility to identify and correct this error. If you can see this as an area for improvement and hold responsibility for it and you still feel it is the customer that isn't working, trust this. Even people who are well aware of their issues may find that sensitive subjects (such as money and exchanging it) can bring up unexpected projections. For example, your customer may feel insecure about a lack of funds and thus perceive your product's worth as too extravagant. Paying what it's worth is not for everyone, and it's important to compassionately understand this about your customer. Despite their best efforts, they may not be capable of engaging in a fair exchange with you. If you experience this, it is your responsibility to no longer exchange with them—and to compassionately communicate why. The health of your business depends on it. It is far too risky to continue engaging in relationships that aren't working for all participants. You can find more detail about ending customer relationships in *Chapter 6*.

5. How Do I Adjust My System?

Incrementally. Empathetically. Layer by layer. This process always begins with understanding the needs of your business—and the needs of your customer—and assessing how well they are currently being met. Recognizing the patterns in these needs, you can intuit how well your system is meeting the goals of your business and determine where accountability, norms, and disclosure can be further enhanced to reinforce your system's integrity. Identifying the holes to be filled requires your empathy, your creativity, and your rationality: empathy to provide context for the problem; creativity to generate insights and solutions; and rationality to analyze and fit solutions to the context. For example, you might use empathy to identify that you need greater accountability in the timeliness of payments. Using creativity, you might generate solutions such as requiring a percentage-based prepayment for products, as well as a final payment, and/or having payments due within seven days of purchase, clearly highlighted on the customer invoice and including any interest that may be accrued on overdue payments. Then you will look at the context of your business and your relationship with your customers, to analyze which of these creative and empathetic solutions best fits your system, and begin to implement them. In the coming chapters we'll explore in detail ways you can implement accountability, norms, and disclosure in your business system, so you'll be able to skillfully identify the best tools to adjust and enhance your system.

ACTION

CHAPTER 4

Co-creating Disclosure

My Truth: Perspective Taking

As an appreciator of money and its value, I like to think I have a healthy skepticism around my own, and others', intentions with money. If I'm not asking for something specific in return for what I am giving, like a set price, I understand it is important to disclose what I'd like to receive in return. Otherwise, I might end up getting something I'd rather not receive. This lesson began to take shape almost immediately when I started to experiment with not setting prices, as I found it was not enough to simply say, "There is no price." Nor was it enough to say, "You decide the price." My customers were clear that they needed more information about the exchange in order to feel comfortable and confident engaging in it. The problem was, before I could provide them with guidance and information on our exchange and how it works I first needed to know what I was offering—and requiring—in the exchange and how to clearly communicate it. This is not necessarily a simple, nor easy, task and it takes experience to execute it well. My customers naturally came to three general conclusions; they saw the lack of price as an opportunity to: 1) get more for less, 2) give and receive fairly, or 3) give more and get more. I also noted that what I disclosed and how I disclosed it helped to influence this perspective. For example, their perspective on generosity was variable and changed depending on their mental and emotional states. However, I could encourage generosity by building trust with them. Once provided with adequate information and a feeling of connection to the product, most customers were balanced in their generosity, but I noted that a few were not. They were not able to step out of their fear and lack to trust their (and my) generosity, even in an encouraging and safe environment. These customers, even with adequate information, would drain our exchanges and create an unsustainable relationship. In the context of money and pricing they shared an often-unconscious perspective that humans are inherently not fair, nor generous. This perspective perfectly reflects their own story about relationships, and more specifically about money and finances, and it justifies their actions in relationships with others. In the context of our exchange, they feared I could never be truly happy with what they give, nor would I feel it's fair. And they would reliably self-fulfill this. The truth was, they (consciously or more often unconsciously) opposed the validity of, the sustainability of, and the authenticity of not setting prices, and they challenged my own authenticity as a seller for choosing it. They had their own issues to work through that were far larger than my pricing approach.

Noting this, I saw it was critical to the integrity of my system that these customers and their behaviour not be included nor accommodated, and I realized I could co-create these conditions through the open sharing of facts and information. In clearly stating the exchange my business desired and required, it attracted the right kind of customers to it. In co-creating this disclosure with my customer, my business drew stakeholders who desired non-zero-sum exchanges and made informed and balanced decisions.

What Disclosure Looks Like

To co-create disclosure in your Pay What It's Worth system and sustain it, you need to allow for the open sharing of facts and information. Sharing information leaves the truth out in the open and allows all stakeholders to make their own informed decisions about the exchange. It is critical to building trust. Disclosure in your system of exchange is about finding your balance with generosity through understanding the value of both timidity and assertiveness in your relationships.

As a seller, disclosure allows you to express the cost of providing your product and the value your product provides, without needing to set a price for it. Creating disclosure supports you in exploring, documenting, and sharing the time, love, resources, and energy you put into your work and its product. It also allows you to find creative ways to share this information with your customers. Disclosure provides buyers with more complete information about the time, energy, love, and resources they are valuing when they determine what to pay for a product. It also allows them to assess, before they make a purchase, if their perspective on the worth of the product is similar to the seller's.

As we move forward, I will continue to use the word "product" to describe the products and/or services you create and sell with your business. Please understand I use 'product' in a larger sense, in that I am speaking to the product of your work and business. A Pay What It's Worth system can be applied just as easily to a business that sells products, as to one that sells services. I, for one, have sold both physical and digital products and services with my Pay What It's Worth system. Similarly, I will be using the word "stakeholders" to describe all people and parties invested in the exchange, including the buyer and the seller. Finally, when I speak of "co-creating" these conditions in your pricing system, I am referring to your ability to shape your business reality through your energy, thoughts, feelings, words, and actions. How you use these powers shapes the world and systems around you. In becoming skillful with co-creating, you'll find you don't need to be pushy or grabby in order to achieve what you desire, as you'll find you're naturally achieving your goals with ease and grace.

The Open Sharing of Relevant Information

How you co-create disclosure in your business relationships will be unique to your system. To support you in identifying opportunities to build and improve disclosure in your systems and relationships, and to provide you with the tools to do so skillfully, let's explore some examples of how I've facilitated open sharing of information in my system of exchange, as well as some examples of how other practitioner of not setting prices have. Remember, disclosure is co-created when we responsibly share relevant information and knowledge with each other. The following examples describe how you can employ disclosure in your business systems, why these tools are useful, and what you need to consider when implementing them.

1. Share Information on the Production of the Product

The intention is: To inform all stakeholders of the materials used in the creation of the product, including the labour needed, as well as the strategy and planning required.

This is co-created with: A focused communication strategy highlighting the resources comprising the product; a means for sharing the process for creating/providing the product (such as through co-creating the product with the stakeholder).

The value is: You make visible the quality—and qualities—of the product.

A real world example is: Online retailer BoingBoing's communication strategy when not setting prices for its digital product bundles is to create an informative webpage that details the qualities of the product—the value it adds and a detailed description of the product and the people who've contributed to creating it.[26] As a Naturopathic Doctor, Dr. Emily Bennett engages with her patients in codesigning their plan for wellness and co-creating solutions with them. This creative process allows for her customers to invest more deeply in the long-term value they are receiving (personal communication, October 18, 2018).

Ask yourself: Do all stakeholders have information and knowledge about the elements of production and the resources that go into creating the product? Are all stakeholders aware of the true costs of providing the product?

2. Share Information on the Structure of the Exchange

The intention is: To create a framework that allows all stakeholders to fairly value the product of the exchange.

This is co-created with: Mutually beneficial boundaries and rules for how the exchange will work and clear definition of what is required and expected of each participant.

The value is: You establish a shared understanding of the relationship.

A real world example is: When I begin working with a new client, I ask for them to cosign our shared agreement (see *My Shared Agreement* in the *Resources)*, a simple two-page document that outlines how our relationship will work, and how I'd like them to value my contribution. In it, I ask them to consider how they value their own time, talent, and contribution, and that of other professionals such as a therapist, a lawyer, and/or a photographer, and to use that sense of value as a framework. When selling digital products in my online store, I clearly outline on the product page a framework for how the exchange will work—I introduce myself and I ask for them to thoughtfully consider how they value the product I've created—and I share what is required of the customer in order to acquire the product. They must offer a value that fairly reflects the worth of the product or the exchange will not take place.

Ask yourself: Does the exchange have clearly communicated guidelines for how all stakeholders need to behave?

3. Share Information on the Intention of the Exchange

The intention is: To make visible the motivations for engaging in the exchange, and to assess if the goals of the buyer and seller mutually align.

This is co-created with: An authentic, engaging brand experience and a communication strategy that consciously mirrors and supports the true intentions of the exchange.

The value is: You connect with what's being given and received.

A real world example is: Aspiration Partners, Inc., an investment firm, allows its clients to determine the management fees they pay each quarter. The fees are not based on the size of the account, nor on how well the investment does, instead, clients are asked to "pay what is fair" for the service they have received. When a client first invests, they select the amount of their initial fee, and they can change this fee anytime and as often as they like via their account dashboard. Aspiration, feeling their fee model is fair to the client, counts on the client being fair to them. Adding to their disclosure, Aspiration is transparent about where their management fees go, and donates a portion of them to charities helping spread economic opportunity.[27]

Ask yourself: Are all stakeholders engaged in a shared goal for the exchange?

4. Share Information
on the Needs of the Exchange

The intention is: To co-create a clear understanding of the requirements of the exchange, and to distinguish these requirements from the *expectations* for the exchange.

This is co-created with: An open environment that supports stakeholders in clarifying and communicating their needs and a transparent experience that supports stakeholders in identifying the value being provided to them—before, during, and after the exchange.

The value is: You meet your needs, and those of the person you're in exchange with.

A real world example is: As a yoga studio, Yoga Village uses their website to clearly communicate their needs for exchanging their product. Their "Pay What You Choose" informational webpage details what their pricing system is, why they employ it, where a client's payment goes, and what the studio needs to succeed.[28]

Ask yourself: Does your system of exchange support all stakeholders in functioning in a grounded, effective way?

5. Share Information
on the Constraints of the Exchange

The intention is: To create awareness of and responsibility to the contributions and limitations of the exchange.

This is co-created with: Open communication and creating opportunities early in the relationship for both participants to give, allowing them to express their perspective on giving, generosity, and value.

The value is: You grow in awareness of what you do and do not want to exchange.

A real world example is: I ask new clients to prepay for our first consulting session together. This gives the client the opportunity to assess the value they place on my contribution and their ability to pay for it, and with the payment, I am able to determine whether I feel my customer's sense of value is fair. If I feel it is not, my system of exchange allows me to compassionately return their payment and decline the exchange, before our working relationship begins. In my online store, I have created a similar system. There is no price attached to my products and I clearly communicate that my customer is to determine what they feel the item is worth and pay accordingly. In my shop backend, I have a reserve system set up that does not allow any purchase offer of less than the predetermined amount for that item (such as $1.00), and gives those buyers who are offering less than this amount the ability to reconsider and resubmit their payment. This reserve system allows me to disclose my constraints in the exchange (I will not accept exchanges where the customer is not being responsible to their role of exchanging value) and it provides me with the ability to compassionately decline any offer that I feel isn't being responsible to our exchange of value.

Ask yourself: Does your system of exchange support being responsible to the shared value of the exchange?

Disclosing A Price

Disclosure can also come in the form of **disclosing value constraints for the exchange**, such as by setting a minimum/maximum price, and/or by setting a suggested price for the product of the exchange. I am listing the approach of setting value constraints separately as I feel it's important to consider carefully *why* this is being done, and if it will benefit all stakeholders of the exchange. For example, some stakeholders will see the minimum price as the fair value to pay and they will pay this minimum price without thought. Is this in line with your intention for the exchange? Setting and stating a minimum/maximum price or suggested price for your product will not benefit your exchanges if it is a decision based out of fear. Is your need to set these limits coming from a place of integrity? If you feel unsure about this, you'll find communicating value constraints only limits the value you receive, rather than ensuring or increasing it. I am well aware that this statement flies in the face of much of the Economic and Management Science theory (as well as opinion) out there. But hear me out. That ideological framework is based upon the assumption that value constraints are the only way to ensure fairness in an exchange. What is missing from this perspective is the understanding that pricing is not only a logic and math-based science but also a language and emotion-based art. These economic theories limit their validity with their basic assumptions of: (a) scarcity in the market, and (b) the market being rational and disconnected from people's emotions. If you come from a perspective of abundance in the market, and a perspective of the market being both rational and emotional, these constraints can feel limiting. If you would like to explore this topic further, please review the Management Science references I've already mentioned, as well as the additional ones found at the end of this book.[29] Should you feel you need to set value constraints, I encourage you to consider very carefully what minimum value or suggested value you truly feel is fair and to use that value only. Don't make it any lower or higher than what you honestly feel is fair. I would additionally recommend that if you choose to state a minimum price, you also state a maximum price for the exchange. If this statement sounds odd to you, explore this. Is it really beneficial to your exchanges to communicate only the minimum you're willing to receive? By stating a maximum as well, you are providing your stakeholders with a complete anchor for their valuation, and better encouraging them to fully consider the value they're receiving.

However, what you may find more helpful than disclosing value constraints in your exchanges is to explore how you value your own product and what it feels like when you engage in both fair and unfair exchanges. Each of your business exchanges is an opportunity for you to explore how you perceive your own worth and the worth of what you are exchanging. Through these observations, you will develop a fuller understanding of your offerings and their fluctuating value, your exchange system, and yourself. With this internal knowledge, you will more clearly communicate your product's value—without feeling you need to put constraints around it. This information will also support you in creating opportunities in your system to decline unfair exchanges before they occur. Through your system of disclosure, you have the potential to develop compassionate ways of ensuring value is fairly recognized and given without setting limitations or expectations around it. For example, you could request that new customers prepurchase or make a deposit on their first purchase. From this exchange, you'll get a sense of how your offering is being valued; should it not feel fair you have an opportunity to compassionately communicate this (and, if needed, return the payment) before the relationship develops further. Another approach that is helpful, especially when an exchange is not person-to-person (for example, online), is to set a reserve price for the exchange. By doing this, you have determined what is not a fair offer for your product, and if a potential customer attempts to purchase your product for less than this reserve price, they will be declined and receive a message encouraging them to reconsider their valuation (or some compassionate and clear language to that effect).

Communicating Value

The value of disclosure in your system of exchange represents this simple truth—to create exchanges with integrity, you need to communicate: I value what I offer. When you don't set a value on what you give and receive (through a set price), you need to communicate this worth in other ways. If you don't, your stakeholders won't know how to value you and your offerings. To build your Pay What It's Worth pricing system, you need to explore and find ways to communicate the value your business provides and the exchange of value it needs. In co-creating disclosure into your system, you'll acknowledge the potential for generosity to be misused, and you'll help shape a system that doesn't promote being overly timid and/or overly assertive in giving and receiving.

CHAPTER 5

Co-creating Norms

My Truth: Necessary Boundaries

When I started to experiment with my new pricing model, I decided I needed to approach it with total openness—at least initially. My education and cultural experience operating in a capital economy, where my economic foundations and goals were primarily built around maximizing my own returns, needed to be set aside so I could explore a different type of economy. To employ the protectionism characterized by capital-based thinking simply didn't make sense in this context. I felt that only by seeing how the model operated without constraints could I fully experiment with and understand it. So, at first, I left my customer free to value my offerings as they saw fit. I provided some structure to payments, but little to no guidance or information on what they were receiving and buying beyond experiencing the product itself. In essence, I let them pay what they wanted. The exchange was based on their personal desires, and my desire to give. Having grown up in a culture where we often feel disconnected from the value and cost of the things we purchase, I found experimenting in this way fascinating and truth-telling. It helped me make the critical connection between responsibility and worth. If setting prices could restrict the value I provided by limiting and fixing it, so too, I soon learned, could not setting prices. It risked making the value being provided, and the cost of providing it, invisible. By not providing my customers with guidance or context, I was not taking responsibility for the exchange or honouring my commitment to receive fair value for my product.

There had always been something about the statement, "Give freely, receive freely" that didn't work for me, but I could never quite put my finger on what it was until I started not setting prices. On one hand, I agreed with the statement: If I give freely, without restraint, I will receive freely, without restraint. On the other hand, I wondered, is giving and receiving in this way really what's best for my business and me? Is it what's best for my customer? Have you ever been given something that is more work to receive than the value you place on it? Have you ever been given something that came with conditions? I learned that what I *really need* is to NOT be totally free. Because the truth is, sometimes, the thing I want to give is something you'd benefit from NOT receiving. Sometimes, I'm unbalanced in my giving. Sometimes, I give for the wrong reasons. I could "give freely, receive freely" without bias, but then I wouldn't be responsible to the whole truth of myself—and of you— that sometimes the things I want to give, you do not need; and sometimes the things you want me to receive, I do not need. Sometimes, our giving isn't helpful or generous. Sometimes it's wise to constrain ourselves.

In leaving the customer totally free (but also alone) in determining the value of the product, I was not being responsible to the value the product was offering, to the costs I had already paid for it, and to the relationship of mutual benefit and trust being built between the customer and me. To maintain my integrity, and create a sustainable business model, I found that it was essential to guide my customer in determining value and to hone my system, using customer feedback, to better communicate that value. Only by co-creating these norms with my customer, could my business continuously assess the health of its exchanges, and improve its boundaries around exchanging with others.

What Norms Look Like

To co-create norms in your Pay What It's Worth system and sustain them, you need to create clear and well-founded rules. Rules and boundaries are helpful as they inhibit our desire to exploit the trust of others, and they create a simple framework for how we are all expected to behave. Defining boundaries is not a fear-based act but rather an act to ensure there is a container for something to take root and grow in. The more self-reinforcing your boundaries are—aka the more you stay within your own boundaries—the less you will find you need to enforce them. The easiest way to create self-reinforcing boundaries is to create boundaries that you can, and need to, live by too. Norms in your system of exchange are about finding your balance with generosity through understanding the value of both availability and security in your relationships.

As the seller, norms allow you to explore, document, and share how you like to communicate with, work with, and be valued by others, and what you are willing to give and receive in your (business) relationships. For the buyer, norms provide a structure for understanding and acting in the exchange, and a guide to fairly valuing and pricing what they are receiving.

Clear and Well-Founded Rules

Like disclosure, how you create norms in your business relationships and systems is uniquely yours to decide. You most intimately understand what your business needs to operate in a sustainable and effective manner. To support you in identifying opportunities to build and improve norms in your systems and relationships, and to provide you with the tools to do so skillfully, let's explore some examples of how I've shaped clear and well-founded rules in my system, as well as how other practitioners of not setting prices have. Remember, norms are co-created when we share in the responsibility of following the rules. The following examples describe how you can create norms in your business systems, why these tools are useful, and what you need to consider when implementing them.

1. Establish Boundaries
Around Assessing Value

The intention is: To set benchmarks for determining value; to encourage your customer to consider their ability to fairly set the value of what they receive and the price they pay.

This is co-created with: A communication strategy that supports and promotes mutual benefit and fairness in the exchange, and supporting your customer, through communication and action, in trusting their ability to fairly value what they are receiving.

The value is: You develop a clear sense of what you feel is fair value for your product, and, in turn, your stakeholders receive a clear sense of it. This encourages engagement with stakeholders who are consciously valuing your offering and discourages engagement with those stakeholders who are not.

A real world example is: In my communication, I consciously do not use language nor logic in the vein of "pay what you can," "pay what you like," "pay what you want," etc., as I feel it does not communicate what I desire from the exchange. Instead, I communicate to my customers that they are to consider the worth of the product and pay accordingly. In this way, I encourage people to consider if they can fairly afford the product I am offering for sale, and I discourage those customers who may act unfairly when given the freedom. Similarly, before I provide my consulting services to a customer, I ask that they read and cosign "Our Shared Agreement," a document I have created to ensure there is a shared understanding of the expectations and goals of our collaboration. You can see an example of *My Shared Agreement* in the *Resources*.

Ask yourself: Does your system clearly communicate its need for, and the necessity of, a fair exchange of value?

2. Establish Boundaries
Around Expressing Value

The intention is: To create an effective and sustainable communication style and approach.

93

This is co-created with: Abundant (not fear-based) logic and language; providing relevant information to all stakeholders about your perceptions of value.

The value is: You learn to communicate in ways that authentically support your product's worth being realized; and your customer receives information on how to accurately reflect this worth with what they give.

A real world example is: As a musician, Amanda Palmer ensures that the communication she creates, and the systems she builds, encourage her customer to consider their relationship to her and what they feel her creations are worth to them personally. Palmer very intentionally uses a language and logic of abundance and generosity, consistently sharing her creative process, as well as the intentions behind her creations, and asking her fans and customers, should they choose to purchase these creations, to pay what they are worth to them. Additionally, Palmer actively speaks and writes on "the art of asking," openly discussing how our personal approach to asking affects the results we receive.[30]

Ask yourself: Do all your marketing systems, including your pricing system, consistently reflect a logic and language of abundance?

3. Establish Boundaries
Around Exchanging Value

The intention is: To create sturdy structures for determining value and exchanging it. To encourage responsibility around fairness and mutual benefit.

This is co-created by: Understanding the value of what you are exchanging and clearly communicating it. Actively supporting your customer in being responsible to the value they are receiving. Exploring the optimal ways for you to give and receive value and actively creating those conditions.

The value is: You encourage your stakeholders to share with you in the responsibility of creating a mutually beneficial exchange, through developing a clear understanding of the value you're offering.

A real world example is: At the Halle Orchestra's "Priceless Classics" concert, patrons were admitted to the theater for a "pay what it's worth" performance with tickets they had not yet paid for, and provided with a playbill that included information about creating and producing the production. At the end of the performance, patrons were asked to determine the worth of the performance they'd watched, and to make a payment of that amount.[31]

Ask yourself: Does your system have a clear structure for receiving payments and for guiding your customers in valuing your offerings?

4. Establish Boundaries
Around Recording Value

The intention is: To create accurate accounting systems.

This is co-created by: Establishing how you will responsibly budget and keep track of your costs, spending, sales, and receipts; determining your systems for billing your customers and providing receipts.

The value is: You develop an effective system for managing your business finances, and your customer participates in and receives clear structures for making payments.

A real world example is: In my business, every customer receives a receipt for their purchase, and the price paid

95

for it is tracked and recorded monthly in my accounting system. Similarly, what I have spent, and the price paid for it, is tracked and recorded. By doing this, I am able to monitor and learn from my historical sales and spending patterns, which supports me in having a grounded understanding of the budget and finances of my business.

Ask yourself: Does your system accurately record and communicate the value you're exchanging?

5. Establish Boundaries
Around Determining Value

The intention is: To communicate expectations around what's being given and received to all stakeholders in the exchange.

This is co-created by: Stating your need for a fair and balanced exchange of value, and enforcing these boundaries compassionately and effectively.

The value is: You develop a clearer understanding of what you realistically need and want to give in your exchanges, and your stakeholders receive a clearer understanding of what you're providing. You support your stakeholders in considering and expressing what they are willing and able to give and receive—before, during, and after the exchange.

A real world example is: When offering their web design services, Hoppel Design provides all potential clients with a complimentary conversation, and a detailed project estimate with timelines, as well as a project price range. These tools allow the firm to explore their potential client's needs, and their understanding of the exchange and their willingness to contribute fairly to it.[32]

Ask yourself: How does your system reinforce your boundaries around generosity, and does it support the consistent creation of non-zero-sum exchanges?

Norms could also look like **establishing payment boundaries for the exchange**, in the form of a payment floor/ceiling (a minimum/maximum price) and/or in the form of a suggested price for the offering. Similar to the previous chapter, I am listing this approach separately as I feel it's important to consider carefully *why* these numeric boundaries are being created, and if they will benefit all stakeholders in the exchange. What do you hope to achieve through this action? Have you considered that suggesting prices may be as harmful to your exchange as it is helpful? Is there a good reason your stakeholder can't fairly determine a fair price without your influence? Rather than providing number-specific payment boundaries, you may want to consider knowing your own value floor for your offerings (see *Chapter 4)* and making it a norm to not engage in relationships where this sense of value is not being matched and exceeded.

Building Strong Connections

The value of norms in your system of exchange represents this simple truth—an abundant life is characterized by stability and sufficiency. Creating a realistic container for your freedom is critical. When you do not set a limit on the value you can give and receive (through a set price), you need to find other constraints for determining value and exchanging it in a sustainable way. If you do not, you will find yourself engaging in zero-sum exchanges with your stakeholders. To build your Pay What It's Worth pricing system, you need to examine and transform your relationships through the establishment of healthy boundaries. In co-creating norms into your system, you'll acknowledge the potential for generosity to be misused, and you'll help shape a system that doesn't promote being overly available and/or overly secure with giving and receiving.

CHAPTER 6

Co-creating Accountability

My Truth: Exploring My Role

I came to understand, through my experience not setting prices, that without information (or context), most people do not know how to fairly value what they are receiving—and they feel uncomfortable trying. While my customers would express appreciation for my adaptable and innovative pricing approach, they also communicated in various ways that they did not, in fact, want that much freedom, and that, in some ways it felt misleading. Because even if I didn't set a price for my creation, I as the creator did have some sense of what was fair value for it. After all, I had already paid something to create and produce the product. I possessed a responsibility for the value I was giving, and it proved vital to my health and that of my business to be accountable to this knowledge by actively expressing it. As well, it became clear that in a business exchange it was important to consistently remind myself that I was never asking my customer to determine what *I* was worth. Even in the context of prostitution or other exchanges where someone is selling their body or physical resources, they are still not selling their self-worth, nor their sense of self. They are selling a product, providing a service. Business exchanges are about the "it," the product of the transaction, the thing of value that can be exchanged. Whether the "it" is my intangible time and talent, or a tangible creation like a book, the "it" is what my customer was after and valued. And the more I was able to see my products and services not as ME, but as expressions of me—and be accountable to this—the easier it was to communicate my product's value, which added to the value I received. It took time to consistently find a place where I felt confident I was communicating clearly about my pricing approach, my product, and the value it provided. In turn, it took time for my clients and their valuations to accurately reflect the worth of what I was offering. Without having a price to attach my value to, I needed experience developing other techniques for communicating value. Only then could I examine the difference between what my fearful logic and language created, and what my more grounded communications created. It became clear that when I was feeling whole and centred in my integrity, my customers mirrored this back to me in their behaviour, namely by how generous they were with their money and love. Similarly, when I used fear and ego in my communications and acted from my feelings of lack, I would misuse my power and sway my customer's valuations, usually in the direction of underpaying for the value they were receiving. With these observations in hand, it became a practice for me to be very conscious about how I communicate about money—making it, spending it, giving it, receiving it—and to examine if it was in a balanced and empowered way. When I found a particular exchange didn't work well and/or it didn't feel fair, I took it as feedback about the system I was designing. What conditions caused more positive and/or negative results? In doing this, I felt I was doing my part to realize–and to be accountable to–the worth of my work.

What I noticed was, the variables of the exchange mattered the most. Similar to doing a chemistry experiment, the elements (or variables) involved–and the way in which they were allowed to interact–determined the result. I, being one of the main variables, and how I interacted, was critical to the results I received. In fact, "I" seemed to matter more than anything else as I noticed my customer's perception of value was very much tied to my recognition of it. As a new business owner and as a young woman, my confidence and talent had room to grow, and not setting prices slowly developed into a tool for highlighting those areas where I was not giving myself enough of the credit I deserved. It seemed the more wholly and authentically I was able to present the value I was offering, the more wholly that value was recognized by my customer. This "whole-ing" took time and space (and my journey's not over yet), but I have reached a place where I understand fully that my lack–and my love–is returned to me, and I am responsible for which one I am sharing with you.

What Accountability Looks Like

To co-create accountability in your Pay What It's Worth system and sustain it, you need an effective system for dealing with violators. The point is not to punish people. It's to establish that there are consequences for acting poorly. Think of accountability as a container for our actions, and fairness is the key to constructing it. Accountability in your system of exchange is about finding your balance with generosity, through understanding the value of both empathy and perspective-taking in your relationships.

As the seller, accountability allows you to trust that you are truly creating a balanced and respectful relationship with your stakeholders where all participants are fairly valued. As the buyer, accountability supports your responsibility in fairly valuing the relationship, and what you're receiving from it—and giving to it.

Accountability highlights an important aspect of service and of well-functioning systems, the critical difference between service and self-abandonment. An example of self-abandonment is prioritizing service to others to such a degree that you martyr yourself to the ideal of service. Despite appearances, finding yourself very attached to what you want and need from providing your service creates a situation where you're actually serving yourself, not others. It's a form of self-absorption and/or self-denigration. Giving so much time, energy, or material goods to a person or cause—more than you can realistically afford—creates a deficit and hardship for you. Being accountable to this, understand you're also responsible for *not* giving away everything you have. This means when you choose to give, you also need to be responsible for compensating for that loss. Being accountable to your service, you'll find everyone benefits from it—the server as well as the served.

The Establishment
of Fair Consequences

Like norms and disclosure, how you create accountability in your business will be unique. You understand
best what your business needs to operate in a sustainable and effective manner. To support you in identifying opportunities to build and improve accountability
in your systems and relationships, and to provide you
with the tools to do so skillfully, let's explore some
examples of how I've established fair consequences in
my system of exchange, as well as how other practitioners of not setting prices have. Remember, accountability is co-created when we share in the responsibility
of behaving well and the consequences of not.

1. Establish a Responsibility to Fairness

The intention is: To establish shared responsibility for fairly
valuing the product of the exchange; to create space for
all stakeholders to compassionately remove themselves
from the exchange should they not be fairly valued.
This is co-created with: A communication strategy
highlighting the importance of mutual benefit and the
shared responsibility of behaving fairly in the exchange.
The value is: You establish a clear boundary and goal
for the exchange: fair value. You support your customer in feeling empowered and confident in their
ability to fairly determine the value of what they are
receiving and the cost for it.
A real world example is: Author Stephen King digitally
released his novel, *The Plant*, by delivering chapter
installments on his website. Readers were asked to pay

$1 for each chapter downloaded, either before or after reading. He pledged to continue writing the novel if at least 75% of his readers complied. At the time he reportedly said: "If you pay, the story rolls. If you don't, the story folds."[33]

Ask yourself: Does your system encourage behaviour that benefits all stakeholders?

2. Establish a Responsibility to Satisfaction

The intention is: To create a system of feedback with your stakeholders.

This is co-created with: Supportive feedback loops that encourage all stakeholders to constructively share their experiences, positive and negative, with your brand.

The value is: You establish a flow of feedback with your stakeholders that will support you in identifying the weaknesses and strengths, opportunities and threats in your business systems, and allow you to improve upon them. You create avenues for feedback to be expressed in ways other than through the exchange of money.

A real world example is: To receive the most accurate customer feedback about their film, the creators of *My Accomplice* asked cinema-goers as they left the theater to pay only what they thought the night (and the film) was worth.[34] ARC Stokton Arts Centre in England employs "pay what you decide" pricing as a means to remove the financial risk their customer must take in buying a ticket for a show in advance of knowing whether they are going to enjoy it or not.[35]

Ask yourself: Does your system ensure satisfaction and delight, and encourage the flow of feedback and innovation?

3. Establish a Responsibility to Value

The intention is: To understand your stakeholders' perception of value in relation to your own. To create an environment where money, value, and the exchange can be explored with freedom.

This is co-created with: Communications that acknowledge your motivations for being generous, and communications that support your needs in exchange with others. Developing a connection with your stakeholders that supports them in feeling safe to talk about topics that may be sensitive.

The value is: You reduce the ability for your offerings to be misused. You support your customer in feeling empowered and confident to share without regress.

A real world example is: Some community acupuncture studios offer their services using a Pay What It's Worth sliding scale, stating the low to high price that can be paid for the product, such as $30 - $75 per session.[36] In Daniel Bye's (2012) *The Price of Everything,* the performance artist explored the idea of value, and using a mix of stand-up and storytelling, invited the audience to speculate on the value of everything from a glass of milk to an air guitar. The audience was also invited to speculate on (and pay) the value they received from the evening.[37]

Ask yourself: Does your system explore, communicate, and preserve the value you are offering?

4. Establish a Responsibility to Consciously Evaluating Worth

The intention is: To communicate respect for your stakeholders, yourself, and your offering.

This is co-created with: Communications modeling a language and logic of abundance. Establishing connection and trust in your relationship with your stakeholders, supporting and guiding them to feel safe to fully experience what they are giving and receiving.

The value is: You ensure your offerings will be respected and rightfully valued. You support your stakeholders in feeling confident and comfortable in your exchange, and in the ambiguity of not having a set price.

A real world example is: In 2015, comedian Louis C.K. decided to not set prices and instead have his fans determine the value and price of one of his stand-up specials. In his communications on the topic, he used the very specific language of "pay what it's worth" when describing what he was asking his customers to do. His communications clearly asked the customer to consciously evaluate the worth of what they were receiving, as he desired to benefit from the exchange, as well.[38]

Ask yourself: Does your system create trust and focus on the mutual exchange of worth?

5. Establish Responsibility Around Ability and Means

The intention is: To support all stakeholders in realistically determining if they can afford to participate in the exchange.

This is co-created with: Information that supports your stakeholders in fairly understanding and determining the value they're considering exchanging.

The value is: You support yourself and all your stakeholders in feeling empowered by and confident in their ability to provide—and be provided with—what they need.

A real life example is: The Real Junk Food Project Birmingham is a group of cafes and restaurants in Birmingham, UK affiliated with The Real Junk Food Project (TRJFP), a global charitable organization whose mission is to intercept edible surplus food from landfill and make it accessible to everyone through a network of pay-as-you-feel cafes. Every Friday, TRJFP Birmingham (a self-sustained Community Interest Company) offers freegan boxes, containing some of the 6 tonnes of food they intercept each week. The company is very clear that the boxes are NOT free, and rather are pay-as-you-feel. They ("What is a freegan box," n.d., para. 5) communicate clearly this means "you contribute however you can to the success of our project: donating your time, skills, money, or something even more imaginative! How you choose to contribute is entirely up to you."[39] They go on to share a host of ideas for how you can use your time and skills to support the project.[40] Through their system for not setting prices, TRJFP Birmingham allows the customer willingness to contribute to determine whether the exchange takes place. The system supports sellers and buyers in clearly communicating what is required to participate in the exchange.

Ask yourself: Does your system promote responsibility?

Ending Relationships

You may find that despite your best effort to co-create trust with your customer, that trust is not sustaining. Should you find yourself in this place, where your relationship feels too risky to continue, I encourage you to trust yourself and your feelings enough to express them—and to be prepared to end the relationship should you feel you need to.

To assist you with expressing dissatisfaction constructively, I encourage you to share with your customer each time you feel they are not being accountable to the relationship. Do not ignore this behaviour and/or make light of it. In your business, you might develop periodic accountability checkpoints. These will allow you to more quickly acknowledge when your accountability standards are not being met. When this happens, the key is to communicate with your customer in a manner that is neutral and clear while acknowledging your responsibility for the situation, as well as your feelings about it. We explored communicating effectively and with neutrality about Pay What It's Worth, money, and mutual benefit in *Chapter 4*. Another preventative approach is to create conditions in your systems that do not give space to this type of zero-sum behaviour in the first place. See *Chapter 5* for more specific support on doing so.

Despite these preventative measures, you may still find you need to end a relationship. Knowing how to compassionately and calmly end relationships is a valuable business and life skill, and while I cannot claim to be an expert on the topic, I have found that a certain formula seems to work. This formula is contingent on not blaming nor shaming the customer, and focuses on the shared risk of the relationship continuing. In action, this may look like communicating your appreciation for your customer's business, while highlighting how the exchange has not worked for your shared relationship. If the customer and/or you has expressed dissatisfaction with the exchange previously you can speak to this.

In providing examples of how this shared trust has already been compromised you are showing the risk of another exchange, and you are guiding your customer in identifying their own need to end the relationship.

Taking Responsibility

The value of accountability represents this simple truth—in order to make good money doing what you enjoy while serving others, you need to identify and remove your negative beliefs and the self-worth and self-sabotage issues holding you back. We all have them. It's your responsibility to realize yours—and to realize that everyone else, and especially your customer, has these issues too. We are all works in progress. To be accountable to this truth, you need to check in on your systems. You need to look at and identify what's not working, explore how the issue could shift with a change in your thoughts and/or actions, then enact these adjustments to bring about the results you desire. To build your Pay What It's Worth pricing system, you need to be open to innovating and to being accountable for the ways you hold yourself and your business back. In co-creating accountability in your system you'll acknowledge the potential for generosity to be misused, and you'll help shape a system that doesn't promote being overly empathetic and/or overly rational with giving and receiving.

CHAPTER 7

It's Your Combination

My Truth: Giving = Receiving

Unknowingly, while I was muddling around and finding my way with my Pay What It's Worth pricing system, I was also learning where I limited myself internally and externally when it came to my relationship with money. My inner learning involved observing and transforming my thoughts, feelings, beliefs, attitudes, and decisions about myself and money, and my outer learning focused on marketing myself, creating opportunities for higher pay, and managing my money. As my inner relationship to money transformed, I naturally applied my learning to my outer relationship to money, which allowed me to shape an economic system that was current and reflective of my growing awareness.

One of my challenges was learning to market myself. This involved getting clearer on my personal brand (what I believe in) and communicating it clearly, while also sharing the value I offer and who can benefit from it. This included looking very closely at how I was selling my products and the means, or system, by which I was not setting prices. In order to operate a thriving abundant business, I needed to communicate like one, and I needed to be watchful of anything that was NOT working in it or for it. Was I being consistent in my communication about the value I was offering? Was I effectively guiding the customer? Was I consistent in communicating with abundance? Today I continue to observe where my marketing can be improved to better align with what I desire to create. To create opportunities for higher pay and to grow my wealth, I did my best to focus on continuously improving my products and services and on creating new offerings and avenues of value. Most importantly, I worked to identify and explore the places where I was preventing myself from wholly realizing my value. This allowed me to find new avenues to grow my wealth in. To manage my money in increasingly effective ways, I worked on the flow of it, its comings and goings, and how they balanced. I explored the most abundant and fair ways of receiving payment for my work and how I could minimize the costs of providing it. A big part of managing my money was guiding and managing my customer's perception of value, as they needed my support in deciding how much money to share with me. In a similar vein, creating a sturdy perception of value supported my customer, and me, in creating a budget and plan in such an untraditional pricing setting. With a sturdy perception of value established, there was a consistency to the price paid, and the demand for it, as well as how these aspects grew over time.

As I've explored with you, Pay What It's Worth evolved to become my most powerful tool for realizing where I needed to transform my own thoughts, feelings, beliefs, attitudes, and decisions about money. Now, each time I have an external difficulty with money, I reflect on my thoughts and actions and how I've contributed to the difficult situation. My customers and their behaviour help me to see where my system of mutual benefit, trust, and exchange is not working—and how I can improve my relationships through transforming my inner world and subsequently my external actions. Similarly, whenever I receive great success and feel highly valued, I take note of why I feel this way, what conditions are present in the relationship, and how I can encourage them further. My feelings around not setting prices—and by association, money, value and myself—have oscillated in the course of my experience and have swung from confident and enthralled to terrified and repelled and back again and everywhere in the middle. At first, there were so many unknowns they were all I could focus on, and while my heart felt firm in its belief in what I was doing, I had moments of wild anxiety where I wondered why the hell I was selling my offerings this way. I wondered if all I was doing was making my life harder. Each time I decided to continue with the practice, and to learn from whatever issue I was encountering, I became more comfortable and confident with not setting value. What kept me with the system was how great I inherently felt using it and how strong the relationships of exchange I was building were. While there were serious moments of difficulty, it was easy to notice how my life and business improved as I worked on my relationships with money and with myself. Reflecting on my past attitudes and decisions around money, I see I entered into my Pay What It's Worth experiment with very little structure and not much of a plan. My curiosity superseded security. My business was brand new and my pricing was just one of the many business systems that was undefined and in the midst of being built. I determined a great metric for my experiment would be whether I had consistent business, if revenue was sustaining my needs, and if my customer's feedback and experience was positive and loyalty-building. I also thought it would best serve what I was exploring if I began my experiment as open to it as possible and added boundaries as needed. The adjustments that followed and the system I use today reflected my ongoing learnings about money, exchanging value, and relationships.

Perceived Value is...

Figure 4. The value they see is the value you feel (own drawing).

What started as an experiment in shifting my thinking around pricing and value, expanded to transform my marketing and my business model, and ended up elevating the way I value others and myself. It proved to be an experiment whose results I could not fully understand until I realized that Pay What It's Worth supported me in feeling whole—and that these feelings were critical to my pricing system being effective. Coming to understand and work with my own fear, I learned to value giving and receiving equally and I learned how it is not helpful, nor healthy, to value one over the other. Poverty, scarcity, and lack are created as much from a resistance to giving as they are to a resistance to receiving. Learning to participate in—and value both equally—is the price I needed to pay to truly feel wealthy, and to be capable of generously sharing that wealth with my world.

Understand Your Generosity

Giving is a web that connects us. Being generous *is* our natural state. It's only because of fear that we have determined it necessary to control and fix the value of things, and ourselves. At its core, money is our tool for investing in people. And we invest well when we're aligned with the same principles that govern natural systems (and man-made systems with integrity). In her article "The Biology of Globalization," Dr. Elisabet Sahtouris (1997, p. 1) writes, "The globalization of humanity is a natural, biological, evolutionary process. Yet we face an enormous crisis, because the most central and important aspect of globalization, its economy, is currently being organized in a manner that so gravely violates the fundamental principles by which healthy living systems are organized that it threatens the demise of our whole civilization."[41] By paying what it's worth and investing in non-zero-sum exchanges, you're investing in our collective wealth, and allowing your current of exchange to align with its natural cycles and rhythms. Discovering what connection, exchange, and mutual benefit looks like in your investments, and how norms, accountability, and disclosure support you in sustaining integrity, you'll find a balance between your values and your wallet.

Giving can be a tangled web of unconscious emotions, impulses, and beliefs, and it's important to honour this truth. It *is* difficult to be generous in a manner that nourishes and sustains. To address this issue from the outside—as changes that must be made by society and by your customers—you first need to look inside, at your own patterns. You need to be aware of your desire to help, to fix, and to save others, as well as your desire to blame them. In order to authentically improve your system, you will need to see every problem as your issue to address. Otherwise, you'll find yourself more concerned with other people's problems than your own, and you'll find yourself disrespecting others by taking on their issues unnecessarily. If your exchanges are to be balanced, with no one giving too much, or for the wrong reasons, you'll need to discover what fair exchanges of value feel like—and insist upon them. You will need to be heroic in your giving. Otherwise you may find yourself on weak financial ground (from giving too much) and/or creating a financial landscape littered with expectation and disappointment (from giving for the wrong reasons). Wisely protect your right to be generous, and your foundations of integrity. Remember, when you encounter a customer who wants abundance without an exchange of services, it is like wanting love without loving. It's simply not of value for anyone.

Transform to Thrive

At its core, business is about relationships. What you need to thrive and sustain in a Pay What It's Worth pricing system is what any value-adding, balanced relationship needs to thrive: An intention to love, value, and respect the other and yourself, expressed through the exchange of information, boundaries, and responsibility. Being conscious of your intention and being conscientious in carrying it out enables you to generate the quality of life you desire. Connection, exchange, mutual benefit—the goal is a sustainable, regenerative economy. When you know what you want to achieve from your system, you can allow yourself to focus on the process without expectations. Expectations are not the same as goals. Goals, like intentions, are what you want to achieve. Expectations are your assumptions about what will happen on the journey towards these goals. When you have expectations, you tend to control situations, and as we have explored, this is not what you need to do. Rather, you need to allow your experiences—not your fears or your expectations—inform and shape your system.

What you create is yours to imagine. The ingredients that go into your Pay What It's Worth system will be a combination uniquely your own. I trust you have the love to transform your relationships, the wisdom to invest wisely, and the power to design systems and relationships that work for you. You have what you need to create exchanges that support your creative passions, and to choose relationships that create the positive impact you desire. May you transform your world with them.

"When we quit thinking primarily about ourselves and our own self-preservation, we undergo a truly heroic transformation of consciousness."[42]

–Joseph Campbell

RESOURCES

An Exploratory Checklist:
Is Pay What It's Worth For You?

Select the statements that apply to you.

I AM:

☐ a business owner focused on creating positive relationships and experiences for my customers.

AND:

☐ I am creating and running a business that is shaped on integrity and shared trust between customer and provider.

☐ I am creating an experience that is based on what my business does AND what my customer does.

☐ I am interested in creating long-term relationships with my customers.

☐ I am focused on creating a great experience for those who interact with my brand.

☐ I feel my brand is reflected in every interaction my customer has with my business and work.

☐ I am prepared for my value to grow gradually over time and I am willing to be patient with this.

I AM:

☐ offering a one-of-a-kind product focused on creating value.

AND:

☐ I resonate with the saying, "do one thing really, really well" (though I may do more than one thing really, really well).

☐ I see my work as unique.

☐ I express my wealth through my gifts.

☐ I do not make decisions based upon profit alone; my larger focus is on value.

☐ I believe that by creating genuine value for others, a sustainable profit will emerge for me.

☐ I am creating a career from my passion, talent, and values and I believe this is my recipe for mental, physical, spiritual, and financial abundance.

☐ I do not believe I could be more wealthy doing something I tolerate, rather than something I am gifted at.

I AM:

☐ building long-term relationships with my customers.

AND:

☐ My customers value me and my value grows over time.

☐ I have designed my business and the service I provide in a way that encourages an ongoing relationship with my customers and fans.

☐ I am happy investing time and energy in slow growth.

☐ I am here to empower my customers; I have no desire to manipulate or control them.

☐ I do not want to use fear as means to drive customers to action.

☐ I feel communication and connection are key to any positive relationship.

☐ I want my customer relationships to be built on something lasting and valuable—mutual trust and respect, and a shared vision.

I AM:

☐ looking to shift my relationship with money.

AND:

☐ I want to be more aware of how I overemphasize and underemphasize its value and importance.

☐ I want to be more aware of when I give and take to excess.

☐ I want to be more aware of when I perceive money as being scarce.

☐ I desire to expand my view of what value means, and how I view my time, contributions, and energy.

☐ I want to create more supportive boundaries around money and remove unhelpful ones.

☐ I desire more open communication about pricing, value, and money.

☐ I believe money is a form of energy that is given and received.

☐ I believe I have a choice in the relationship I have with money.

I AM:

☐ exploring how I can further support my material growth.

AND:

☐ I want to find the sweet spot on the supply/demand curve where my price, the demand, and what I can supply are in equilibrium.

☐ I do not desire for the market alone to signal to me when I need to increase/decrease my prices.

☐ I believe market prices alone are not a reliable source for determining my value to others.

☐ I feel I do not need to have a set price for my work. I'm willing to allow demand and my customer's experience to determine the value of my work.

☐ I believe that the value of my work is variable, changing with the customer's needs.

☐ I see my work as my art, and I want it to be valued that way.

☐ I want to be clearer in my communication around money and value.

I AM:

☐ exploring how I can further support my spiritual growth.

AND:

☐ I want to support myself in discovering how my relationship with money may be blocking my growth.

☐ I am ready and willing to address and work on my own issues around money and value.

☐ I am willing to uncover how I undervalue and overvalue myself, and work to find equilibrium where my authentic value lies.

☐ I am aware that if any issues arise using Pay What It's Worth pricing they will be a reflection of my own issues around money and self-worth, and are an opportunity for me to examine my preconceived notions.

☐ I believe if and when I truly value myself and my offerings, what I receive from Pay What It's Worth will be greater than any limitation I place on it.

☐ I believe communication and compassion are the key to any problem I may encounter with Pay What It's Worth.

I AM:

☐ exploring how I can further support my emotional growth.

AND:

☐ I desire to deepen my connection to my customers by cultivating a relationship of trust and value.

☐ I do not desire connections with my customers that are not mutually beneficial.

☐ I love the idea of building more trust in my customer relationships and fostering the belief that we are both there to do the best we can.

☐ I am ready to receive feedback on how I value myself through the value set by my customers.

☐ I am prepared to fortify and communicate my boundaries if I find a customer taking advantage of my pricing flexibility.

☐ I understand my own feelings about my value are the largest hindrance to me not being fairly valued.

I AM:

☐ exploring how I can further support my intellectual growth.

AND:

☐ I believe that the principles of our economy are flawed and have been built on some faulty assumptions. I'm interested in exploring this.

☐ I am interested in what I can learn when someone values my work.

☐ In exchanges I want to operate from a mindset of "what can I give?" and not "what can I get?"

☐ I want to observe how my own personal economy changes when I approach things from a perspective of "what can I give?"

☐ I want to observe how my personal economy changes when I choose to engage in equal value exchanges, neither undervaluing nor overvaluing myself or others.

☐ I know that any pricing system I use will not be perfect or without flaws.

I AM:

☐ Not interested in restricting the growth of my customers.

AND:

☐ I feel I do not need to tell my customers how to value my service. They are aware of what they receive from me.

☐ I trust that my customers can determine when they do not have the means or ability to value my work fairly.

☐ I do not want to consciously or unconsciously apply fear or scarcity tactics in my marketing communications, including those around pricing.

☐ I believe that investing in my customer's growth will result in my own growth.

☐ I trust my customers to communicate how they value me.

☐ If my customers' "money stuff" comes up during our exchange, I can empathetically determine if I feel comfortable continuing to offer them service.

☐ I will not caretake nor enable my customer's "money stuff." Our relationship is about an equal value exchange.

I AM:

☐ Not interested in restricting the growth of my business.

AND:

☐ I want to remove price as a major barrier to entry, and to business growth.

☐ I want my business growth to develop from the value created by my work.

☐ I do not want to put limits on what my contribution could be worth to another.

☐ I am accepting of the fact that some people value my work more and others less.

☐ I do not believe everyone is my ideal customer and I feel my pricing can be used as a tool to attract my ideal client.

☐ I have a sense of what fair value is for my work.

☐ I want my financial growth to be affected by factors other than myself, and the market.

☐ I am interested in how price and pricing affects business relationships.

I AM:

☐ Not interested in restricting my own growth.

AND:

☐ I want to explore my thoughts and feelings around value and money.

☐ I want to understand how I view my own value and how that affects how my customers view my value.

☐ I want to become more conscious of how I value others and their contributions.

☐ I want value to be my motivator for buying and selling, rather than the price.

☐ I'd like to see more clearly how my ideas and attitudes around money affect my business and my life.

☐ I want to be more conscious of my scarcity and fear-based thinking around money.

☐ I don't want to control the monetary value placed on my service. I want to allow my value to grow and flow as it will.

☐ I desire a stronger sense of my self-worth.

Having reviewed the checklist and your level of agreement with it... Do you feel you identify with the Pay What It's Worth perspective on creating wealth?

A Model to Expand From: My Pay What It's Worth System

My system has shifted and changed as I've grown to understand how I want to invest in connection, exchange, and mutual benefit. This is what it looks like...

My intention is to be:

- Engaging in fair and sustainable exchanges where my customer and I are mutually investing in the long-term value and growth of our connection.

Co-creating disclosure in my system looks like:

- Engaging my customer in the creation process as much as possible; through co-creative and collaborative service offerings, supportive listening, and the sharing of my journey and experience—through one-to-one and social (media) communications;

- Creating information tools that share the value and costs of the product or service I've created and is being sold;

- Encouraging my customer to have an open dialogue with me about money, worth, and value;

- Communicating compassionately and in a timely manner if I feel I am not being valued fairly and/or when I need to leave a business relationship.

Co-creating norms in my system look like creating clear and simple payment structures from which the customer can value the product or service:

- In my general system, invoices and receipts are issued and sent to my customer promptly; payments from my customer are due immediately; I do not state a minimum or suggested $ value for anything I sell; I am clear in my language and logic that I am seeking an exchange of mutual benefit;

- In my service system, I communicate that my time and contribution is the item to be valued, and that before I give my time and talent, my customer needs to pay for this contribution; I suggest determining the value one places on their own time and talent, or a similar professional when valuing my time and contribution; I keep my customer updated on the time and tasks I've contributed;

- In my product system, I communicate that the work is the item to be valued; I provide demonstrations of the product before purchase as well as information on what's being purchased, including the costs and the intrinsic value of it; if physical, I share the material costs of making the product to ensure they are covered with the purchase price.

Co-creating accountability in my system looks like:

- Encouraging written and verbal feedback about what has been given and received and the level of satisfaction with it;

- Communicating my pricing in a manner that encourages shared responsibility to the exchange being fair and sustainable;

- Acting with emotional and financial sensitivity and responsibility;

- Not engaging in exchanges that are not fair and sustainable;

- Being aware of and continuously working with my beliefs and feelings around money, value, and worth.

My Shared Agreement (for Providing Service)

In my Pay What It's Worth system for providing business services, this is the agreement I have every new customer sign. This agreement is intended to be morally binding only.

Our Shared Agreement

This document outlines our shared commitment to consciously working together.

In signing this document, you agree to do your best to consciously create a fair and balanced business relationship. You agree to the mutually beneficial principles outlined (below), and you agree to do your best to continuously honour and respect the *Shared Goals*, *Shared Values*, and *Shared Investment* of our business relationship. As well, you are open to (giving and receiving) feedback on these shared principles.

Our Shared Goals

To ensure success in our work, we commit to:

1. Sharing essential information.
2. Creating motivation to inspire action.
3. Elevating our credibility with our professionalism and integrity.
4. Supporting our brand through our values.

Our Shared Values

To support our relationship, we commit to:

1. Mutual respect; honouring each other's needs.
2. Trust and honesty.

3. Open, authentic conversations.
4. Accountability; sharing responsibility.
5. Continuous learning; personally and professionally.
6. The creativity of each of us; helping each other to build creative confidence.
7. Generating results and reaching goals.
8. Investing in each other's wealth.

Our Shared Investment

To grow in our mutual wealth, we commit to:

1. Being fair to the value of our collaborative relationship.
2. Respecting each other and the contribution we provide.
3. Treating each other as the consummate professionals we are.
4. Doing our very best for each other, and our project.
5. Fairly evaluating the time and contribution we each provide.
6. Respecting the stated policies around billings and payments.
7. Honouring the shared responsibility we hold towards working together successfully.
8. Investing in the satisfaction and benefit of all participants.

_____   _____
     Your Name,   Tara Joyce,
     Co-creator   Co-creator

Running Your System: (Some) Digital Tools For Not Setting Prices

Visit paywhatitsworth.com/tools for up-to-date information.

ACKNOWLEDGMENTS

I *knew* this to be true... but now I *know* it to be true: writing a book is not easy. It's like putting together a puzzle without the box cover-art to guide you. At points, you think you may have a complete picture coming together, and at other times you feel like it's just a big jumbled up mess. To be able to work through this chaos and to write my first book, is my biggest dream realized, and it feels fitting that the help of others proved so critical in realizing it. As someone whose ego loves to assert my ability to do *everything* myself, it is so refreshing and vulnerable for me to take this space to acknowledge the village of people who've helped to make this book possible. Many times in the process of creating this book, I've felt I could not do it, did not want to do it, and/or simply wouldn't do it. I've wanted to back away and to give up. The help and support I've received from others has been absolutely critical in calming this tumultuous relationship and in making this book a reality.

Thank you to my husband, Daniel Bida, and my dearest colleague, coach, and friend, Teya Sparks. Without the two of you pushing me and guiding me to (healthily) push myself, I know I would never be where I am today. Thank you for believing in me and my ability to never stop until I reach my goal.

To my parents, Margaret and Bill Joyce, thank you for all you have taught me. You are invaluable mirrors to learn from and this book would not exist without you.

To my darling Garbo (Gabi Syberg-Olsen), you are my soul sister and my first love, and I'd likely have lost my damn mind a long time ago without you in my world. Thank you for being my partner, and for always accepting me as I am.

Kathryn Willms, you are an editing wizard and I want you to live in my back pocket. Thank you for your thoughtful and invaluable guidance and for helping to shape my wild ramblings into a book I am truly proud of. Your support has meant more to me than perhaps I know how to express with words. Similarly, Greg Ioannou, thank you for knowing the kind of help I needed (and that I needed Kathryn's) when I arrived at your office. You provided the crucial piece I needed to complete this literary puzzle.

Brenda Morgan, thank you for your early encouragement of this manuscript and for your help beginning to shape it into what it is today. Your support gave me the jump-start I needed.

Maria Moriarty, thank you for your support in getting this manuscript and its references into proper

APA format. I would have been lost in a sea of incomplete citations without you. And to Joanna Morrison, thank you for connecting Maria and I. Your generosity, love, and support is so very appreciated.

Arjenna Strong, thank you for your support of my work, for your tireless fascination with alternative-economy businesses, and for creating the Pay What? online guide (http://paywhatonlineguide.weebly.com/). The guide is an invaluable resource for me to learn about (more) alternative-economy businesses, and such a great help while I wrote the real world examples found in *Chapters 5-7* of this book.

To my customers and clients, thank you for your openness and for all you have taught me about building trust and creating fair relationships.

Finally, I want to extend a humongous thank you to the wonderful and generous financial and emotional supporters of this book who've helped to fund its writing. Your investment in this book, and in me, provided me with the fuel I needed to realize this journey. Thank you, Ann Behnke, Sharonna and Jonathan Bida, Yanna and Ayal Bida, Fred Buzzeli, Michelle Schroer, Kristina Cooper, Christine and Mark Dunlop, Erin Fawcett, Josh Gitalis, Jaclyn Greenburg and Daniel Eisen, Margaret and Bill Joyce, Nathalie Lussier, Ebele Mogo, Ken Polak, Lisa Ricci, Fady Sbeih, Ilan Shahar, Alicia Simmons, Adam Singer, Pam Stenberg-Abrahamsson, Gabi Syberg-Olsen, Casey White, and Mandy Wintink. Thank you for believing in me when, quite honestly, I wasn't really believing in myself. Your generosity, and your willingness to share it with me, has made all the difference.

And because I have this space to thank people who mean a whole lot to me, thank you, Gillian Anderson, Chris Carter, and David Duchovny, for co-creating the most dope TV show to ever walk the face of the earth. Well before Pay What It's Worth ever blew my mind, you guys did.

FOOTNOTES

[1] Atkinson, W,W, writing as Three Initiates. (2011). *The kybalion: The definitive edition* (p. 311). P. Deslippe (Ed.). New York, NY: Penguin Group.

[2] Maddox, R. (1995). *Inc your dreams.* New York, NY: Viking USA.

[3] Dignan, P. (2007). *Secrets of the wealthy mind* (pp. 69-71). Denver, CO: Outskirts Press.

[4] Von Neumann, J., & Morgenstern, O. (1944). *Theory of games and economic behavior.* Princeton, NJ: Princeton University Press.

[5] Grazer, B. (Producer), & Howard, R. (Director). (2001). *A beautiful mind* [Motion picture]. United States: Universal Pictures.

[6] Wright, R. (2009). *The evolution of god* (p. 200). New York, NY: Little, Brown and Company.

[7] Collins, K. (2014). *The nature of investing: Resilient investment strategies through biomimicry* (p. 13). Brookline, MA: Bibliomotion.

[8] Carnegie, D. (1981). *How to win friends and influence people* (3rd ed., p. 210). New York, NY: Simon and Schuster.

[9] Bernasek, A. (2009). *The economics of integrity: From dairy farmers to Toyota, how wealth is built on trust and what that means for our future* (pp. 142-145). New York, NY: HarperCollins Publishers.

[10] Isaac, R.M., Lightle, J.P., & Norton, D.A. (2010). *The pay-what-you-like business model: Warm glow revenues and endogenous price discrimination.* Tallahassee, FL: Department of Economics, Florida State University. Retrieved from http://dx.doi.org/10.2139/ssrn.1612951

[11] Gneezy, A., Gneezy, U., Nelson, L.D., & Brown, A. (2010, July 16). Shared social responsibility: A field experiment in pay-what-you-want pricing and charitable giving. *Science. 329*(5989), 325-327.

[12] Sinek, S. (2009). *Start with why* (p. 80). New York, NY: Portfolio.

[13] Grant, A. (2013). *Give and take: A revolutionary approach to success* (p. 5). New York, NY: Viking USA.

[14] Grant, A. (2013, April). In the company of givers and takers. *Harvard Business Review, 91*(4), 90-97.

[15] Wilber, K. (2007). *The integral vision: A very short introduction to the revolutionary integral approach to life, God, the universe, and everything.* Boston, MA: Shambhala.

[16] Soros, G. (1997, February). The capitalist threat. *The Atlantic Monthly, 279*(2), 45-58.

[17] Hawken, P. (2010). *The ecology of commerce: A declaration of sustainability* (2nd ed., p. 18). New York, NY: Harper Collins.

[18] Hubbard, B. (2015). *Conscious evolution: Awakening the power of our social potential* (2nd ed., p. 91). Novato, CA: New World Library.

[19] Hubbard, B. (2015). *Conscious evolution: Awakening the power of our social potential* (2nd ed., p. 101). Novato, CA: New World Library.

[20] Ray, P.H., & Anderson, S. (2000). *The cultural creatives: How 50 million people are changing the world.* New York, NY: Three Rivers Press.

[21] Wilber, K. (2006). *Integral spirituality: A startling new role for religion in the modern and postmodern world.* Boston, MA: Integral Books.

[22] Hubbard, B. (2015). *Conscious evolution: Awakening the power of our social potential* (2nd ed., p. 67). Novato, CA: New World Library.

[23] Hubbard, B. (2015). *Conscious evolution: Awakening the power of our social potential* (2nd ed., p. 67). Novato, CA: New World Library.

[24] Maslow, A. (1954). *Motivation and personality.* New York, NY: Harper & Brothers.

[25] BrainyQuote.com. (n.d.). *Warren Buffett quotes.* Retrieved from https://www.brainyquote.com/quotes/warren_buffett_149692

[26] Boing Boing. (2018). *Pay what you want.* Retrieved from https://store.boingboing.net/collections/pay-what-you-want

[27] Aspiration Partners, Inc. (2018). *Pay what is fair.* Retrieved from https://www.aspiration.com/pay-what-is-fair/

[28] Yoga Village (n.d.). *Pay-what-you-choose (PWYC).* Retrieved from http://www.yogavillage.ca/pay-what-you-choose.html

[29] Fernandez, J., & Nahata, B. (2009, April 21). Pay what you like. Retrieved from http://dx.doi.org/10.2139/ssrn.1433845; Kim, J., Natter, M., & Spann, M. (2009, January). Pay what you want: A new participative pricing mechanism. *Journal of Marketing, 73*(1), 44-58. Retrieved from https://doi.org/10.1509/jmkg.73.1.44

[30] Popova, M. (2014, November 11). Amanda Palmer on the Art of Asking and what Thoreau teaches us about accepting love

[Blog post]. Retrieved from https://www.brainpickings.org/2014/11/11/amanda-palmer-the-art-of-asking-book/

[31] Service, T. (2015, July 21). The Hallé's Priceless Classics – how much is an orchestral concert worth? You decide. *TheGuardian.com*. Retrieved from https://www.theguardian.com/music/tomserviceblog/2015/jul/21/the-halle-priceless-classics-orchestra-concert

[32] Hoppel Design. (2018). *What is trust-based pricing?* Retrieved from https://hoppel.design/faq/what-is-trust-based-pricing/

[33] Stott, J. (2015, April 18). In the café where you can pay what you want, what would you choose? *TheGuardian.com*. Retrieved from https://www.theguardian.com/money/2015/apr/18/cafe-pay-what-you-want-intercepted-ingredients

[34] Crack, C. (2015, July 16). Pay what you think it's worth film to be shown at the Kirkgate Centre. *CumbriaCrack.com*. Retrieved from https://www.cumbriacrack.com/2015/07/16/pay-what-you-think-its-worth-film-to-be-shown-at-the-kirkgate-centre/

[35] ARC, Stockton Arts Centre. (2018). *Pay what you decide*. Retrieved from http://arconline.co.uk/other/news/pay-what-you-decide

[36] Six Degrees Health. (2015). *Fees*. Retrieved from http://sixdegreeshealth.ca/fees/

[37] Bonham, R. (Director). (2012, August 25). *The Price of Everything* by Daniel Bye, [Programme]. Northern Stage at St Stephen's, Edinburgh.

[38] Romano, N. (2015, August 8). Louis C.K. releases new show online, asks fans to pay whatever they think it's worth. *Time.com*. Retrieved from http://time.com/3989789/louis-c-k-live-at-madison-square-garden/

[39] The Real Junk Food Project Birmingham. (n.d.). *What is a freegan box?* (para. 5). Retrieved from https://trjfpbrum.com/freegan-boxes/what-is-a-freegan-box/

[40] The Real Junk Food Project Birmingham. (n.d.). *Volunteer*. Retrieved from https://trjfpbrum.com/volunteer/

[41] Sahtouris, E. (1997, September). The biology of globalization. *Perspectives in Business and Global Change, 11*(2), 1-17. Retrieved from http://www.sahtouris.com/pdfs/BioGlobalization.pdf

[42] Campbell, J., & Moyers, B. (2nd ed., 1991). *The power of myth* (pp. 154-155). New York, NY: Anchor Books.

ABOUT THE AUTHOR

Unfulfilled at 26, Tara Joyce left her corporate marketing career to start her own business and to explore how she wanted to be of service. Quickly, she was attracted to the seemingly backwards strategy of not setting a price and to allowing her customers to determine the value of her offering, and to sharing what she learned through her blog, *Rise of the Innerpreneur*. Today, the "Pay What It's Worth" concept and Tara's published work support people globally in exploring their own scarcity and fear-based ideas around money, value, and business relationships. Tara lives in Peterborough, Canada with her husband, daughter, and canine son.

Visit her @ elasticmind.ca.